Taekwondo S

JUL 0 9 2004

Acknowledgements

Once again, the authors have come to realize that writing a book is always a collaborative effort. We would like to take this opportunity to thank everyone who has helped and supported us in putting this book together.

* Markus Krechel, 1. Dan Ashihara Karate, 2. Dan Ju-Jitsu, for his assistance as a model (attacker) in the photos.
* Judith Vetter (cover) and Michael Dautzenberg for their photographic work.
* Florian Erb, 3. Dan, Aikido teacher, for the use of his beautiful dojo.
* The companies S+L and KUNTAO, who readily provided us with the suits and equipment used in the photos.
* Simon Dakin, 2nd Dan Taekwondo, for his translation.
* From Meyer & Meyer publishing house: Mr. Hans-Juergen Meyer for giving us the opportunity to realize this project; chief editor Thomas Stengel and our own editor Kai Faltin for their extensive co-operation.

Thank you very much!

The authors

Jürgen Höller/Axel Maluschka

Taekwondo Self-defense

Meyer & Meyer Sport

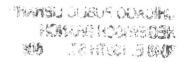

Original Title: Taekwondo Selbstverteidigung – Grundlagen, Trainingspraxis, Gürteltraining
Jürgen Höller, Axel Maluschka
– Aachen : Meyer und Meyer, 2003
Translated by Simon Dakin

British Library Cataloguing in Publication Data
A catalogue record for this book is available from the British Library

Taekwondo Self-defense
Jürgen Höller / Axel Maluschka
Oxford: Meyer & Meyer Sport (UK) Ltd., 2004
ISBN 1-84126-134-3

© 2004 by Meyer & Meyer Sport (UK) Ltd.
Aachen, Adelaide, Auckland, Budapest, Graz, Johannesburg,
Miami, Olten (CH), Oxford, Singapore, Toronto
Member of the World
Sports Publishers' Association (WSPA)
www.w-s-p-a.org
Printed and bound by: FINIDR, s. r. o., Český Těšín
ISBN 1-84126-134-3
E-Mail: verlag@m-m-sports.com
www.m-m-sports.com

CONTENTS

Foreword

I have waited with great anticipation to see where Sensei Hoeller would go with his next book.

I found his previous work an excellent reference work, it was easy to follow, and whilst not dealing with simple concepts, it laid out in fine detail the basic technique, the lines of movement, the target areas, and most importantly of all for the Sensei/teacher, a great deal of variation, and the best way to adapt each technique. Sensei Hoeller has trained in our little Dojo in Dublin, and I have to say I was most impressed with his depth of knowledge and his abilities not only to perform, as any good sensei should be capable of doing, but his depth of knowledge, and his ability to relate to both Sensei and student, which in the present day, is a rare commodity indeed.

He has a sense of humor, and this makes it easy to relate to him as a student/Sensei, and he can be deadly serious, in every sense of the word, when dealing with his passion, the Martial Arts.

He has an inspired insight to the needs of the student, and has gone to great pains in his work, to make the learning of very difficult technique, and understanding of very difficult concepts, as simple as possible for the student, and as deep as possible for the knowledgeable Sensei.

It is very difficult, in the light of modern perceptions of the Martial Arts, to put across the idea that, while Budo may teach you the mechanics of destruction and death, that is not what the Martial Arts are about. If it were, any street thug would be classed as a "master". As any street thug is worth, in combat, their black belt.

The difference between the Martial Artist who trains for leisure time activity, and the street brawler, is that the Martial Artist is living to fight, while the street brawler, for the most part, has spent their life, fighting to live. And life is the greatest prize of all.

The purpose of the Martial Arts is the preservation of life, your own, or someone else's, in a time of dire danger. Using the skills taught.

But there is also the need within humankind to compete, to vie with his/her equal for supremacy. and this competitive urge can be very easily perverted, as many unscrupulous Martial Artists have proven in the past.

But in the hands of a properly trained Sensei, teaching students in the correct manner, and this differs from person to person, the Martial Arts can be done in a competitive format, as long as the main perspective is never lost, once there are rules, it is competition, not actual combat.

In actual combat, there are no rules, no referee, no officials, just the bare facts, once the onset is initiated, you have approximately 10 seconds to live or die. If you survive the first 10 seconds, then chances are you will come out of it relatively unharmed, hurt but wiser.

This does not make good cinema, which has not really done the Martial Arts any favors. but the fact is, a fight for real, in the street, will last about 10 seconds. And not 10 minutes. So, as Martial Artists, we are all training to be 10 second warriors.

And Sensei Hoeller has the grasp of the fundamentals, regarding the passing on of the skills to excel, not in any one Discipline of Martial Arts, but that so rare commodity, an ability to cross the divide, demonstrating universal principles, which can apply to any discipline, or all of them, using that most wonderful human tool, our imagination.

I find that there are very few "new" techniques to learn, once you get past a certain point, but it is a fact that works like this can open doors, and show new ways of doing the same thing.

Even techniques that, as a Sensei, you have taught for many, many years, in a specific way. And to a Sensei, this discovery of a new way, can be as important as hours of blind experimentation, in developing new skills.

It is difficult, once you have passed the point of training directly under a Sensei, to see fresh points of view, and sometimes, not always, the new perspective comes from outside your own style or system.

I found this, when my own Sensei passed away, in April of last year, and the gulf left, almost destroyed me as a Martial Artist.

It is only when your Sensei is gone, you realize how much of your life they filled.

I believe we are the last generation that will see, or practice the Martial Arts/Ways as they were, the insurance companies, and the other vested interests will see to the demise of the Martial Arts in the short term.

Therefore, those who have the knowledge, now, should be treasured.

It is easy enough to ghost write something that looks and sounds good, but it is a rare thing indeed, to find a person who can write about what they do, and actually put the action, to the word, Sensei Hoeller is such a man.

With my compliments, Sir.
Joe Carslake,
8th Dan Hanshi,
Kyushoshinjitsu Ju-Jutsu.

1   PREFACE

Just what is it that drives people to take up a new sport – and in particular – a martial art such as Taekwondo? The exercise, which can compensate for the demands of everyday life; the longing for a healthier lifestyle; the social aspects; the opportunity for self-awareness and self-expression etc etc etc. These are all common motives. When starting training in martial arts there are also the esoteric and mystical factors which many people associate with Asian martial arts. Apart from the reasons mentioned above, *the most important motive*, however, for most people to start martial arts training is *to be able to defend themselves*. Interestingly enough, many clubs and schools do not take this fact into account because of their *tendency towards competition* and due to the fact that Taekwondo, to a large extent, is seen predominantly as a competition sport, many aspects of self-defense are pushed further and further into the background. In doing this we are, on one side, moving away from the roots of a martial art which lie in the ability to fight and to defend oneself and on the other side we are excluding potentially large target groups such as women and the elderly. Self-defense – next to competition, *the* most applicable fighting system in the martial art of Taekwondo- offers these target groups an *interesting, alternative sphere of activity* next to the typical model fighting systems (Kibon, forms, stylized partner training) and competition. Only in doing this can Taekwondo be legitimately referred to as both a lifetime sport and a *martial art*!

In observing normal training sessions and promotion tests, the following facts are evident:

▶▶ Neither student nor instructor recognizes the difference between competition and self-defense.
▶▶ Methods for training self-defense are inadequate.
▶▶ Frustration and the feeling not to have found what was originally wanted lead to a high drop-out rate especially among the above-mentioned target groups.
▶▶ On promotion tests, self-defense is limited to a "walk-on part". And what is more, many of the techniques demonstrated range from the unrealistic to the ridiculous right through to the downright "suicidal".

This book cannot and is not intended to be a "magic formula" to put right all of these problems. It's objective will have been reached if it makes the reader think about the criteria for making his own self-defense solutions more realistic as well as providing enjoyment in practicing the various methods demonstrated. It would be even better, if on top of this, the reader develops an *awareness for the significance of one of the most fundamental fighting systems in Taekwondo* and its *equal importance to the competition fighting system*.

2   The Difference between Competition (Kyorugi) and Self-defense (Hosinsul)

The applicable fighting systems of Taekwondo, *Kyorugi* and *Hosinsul* form the end of a development gained through training fighting systems from the model areas. In the model areas students should work through concepts, theories and basic patterns of movement whereby the emphasis of the individual model systems (*Kibou*, **partner training**, *Poomse*, ...) are trained separately. These elements can then be integrated into the applicable systems. The integration of these model elements is only possible, however, when the model techniques (= basic techniques) are adequately transferred to the corresponding applicable fighting system. The most striking difference is the gap between basic and competition techniques. Over past thirty years, this has lead to a disappearance of the *Hosunsil* system from the whole Taekwondo system and among many Taekwondoka as well as the general public, it has lead to the association of only the *Kyorugi* system with the martial art of Taekwondo. For this reason, many people consider the whole model area of self-defense to be old-fashioned and neglect it during training. It is also worth pointing out that the drop-out rate after the tournament careers of those who train only for competition is higher than that of the people who train all aspects.

In Hosinsul, the unrealistic transfer of (idealistic) model techniques leads to frustration because certain factors such as guarding, agile leg work etc are not taken into consideration. The result of this is unrealistic self-defense techniques which can, at least, be "admired" at promotion tests.

Both fighting systems seem ignorant to the fact that *techniques must be adapted to suit the functions of each of these systems* and that successfully generated model techniques can provide a good basis for this (though this is not always the case as, for example, kick boxing shows how it is sometimes possible to train for competition without any kind of model basic techniques). With the position of Taekwondo as a martial art, the longer route is accepted.

Another mistake is in thinking that competition techniques can be transferred and used just as effectively in self-defense along the lines of "a good tournament fighter will always be able to defend himself on the street". This may sometimes be true but most of the time, also in extreme situations, this is mostly not the case! In the authors' opinion the demands are technically and mentally too different.

There are, of course, some overlaps. People with sparring experience move differently and they can also "take a punch", something that someone without this experience would find difficult. Due to the reduction in techniques in modern Taekwondo (extensive "reliance" on leg techniques) the "tools" to be able to react successfully at close distance are no longer available . In the following comparison some of the fundamental differences between Kyorugi and Hosinsul are demonstrated.

Table 1

Differences between Kyorugi and Hosinsul

Factors of fighting	Kyorugi	Hosinsul
Duration	Mostly 2-3 rounds. With breaks = several minutes.	3-10 seconds.
Techniques	Only a few scoring techniques	More techniques needed than in competition.
Rules	Rules for protection of the fighters.	No rules!
Protective equipment	"Head, groin, forearmand shin protectors"	None!
Distances	"Neutral distance, kicking distance"	All five Distances
Technique	Speed orientated	Speed- but more power orientated
Environment	"Defined: Fighting Area, light conditions, floor, dobok, support by the coach, audience."	
Risk factor	Body and life are not threatened.	Worst case: Injury or death.
Legal factors to consider	No sanctions.	Breaking any laws regarding self-defense. Distorted perception of witnesses
Determination	Good if you have it. If not => defeat without consequence	No determination => No chance!
Killer instinct	Disqualification!	Excellent! (whilst remaining within the limits of the law)
Victory	"Nice medals, acclaim."	"Ripped or damaged clothing. Adrenaline coming out of the ears, possibly trouble with the police."

Note: In a self-defense situation both sides always lose no matter how the confrontation ends!

Therefore: Avoid such situations wherever possible!

3   The basic Principles of Self-defense

3.1   Maximal Response and optimal Solution

If we think of self-defense as a kind of conversation, the attacker is the person asking the questions to which the defender must have suitable answers at hand. The spectrum of possible "answers" (=solutions to the self-defense situation) ranges from ineffective, unsuitable solutions (e.g. random lashing out) to reactions or measures which cause serious injury to the opponent or even death. The defender's perception should, ideally, be so well developed that he can make a realistic evaluation of the situation and can react in the appropriate way. However, there is a whole range of factors which can make evaluation of the situation very difficult or sometimes even impossible.

Time Pressure

Most attacks come unexpectedly. This means that the defender has no time to make conscious decisions. The patterns and behavior picked up during training will come into play or due to the surprise, extreme stress and unfamiliar surroundings the defender may not be able to call upon these skills. This means that in training it is not enough to learn to be able to react with lots of time in a comfortable, familiar environment but that as technical ability increases, *time pressure* should also be increased in self-defense training.

Unexpected Escalation of the Situation

For a better understanding, consider the following: bad light; slippery, uneven ground; limited space; restrictive clothing (ever tried to get through a narrow aisle with a rucksack or a heavy winter coat?); obstacles making self-defense difficult such as fighting in an apartment or on stairs.

All of these factors in some way change, or make impossible, the techniques which can be used.

Adrenalin Rush

The release of adrenalin (a stress reaction!) brings about changes in perception such as tunnel vision, a subjective slowing-down of the situation and physical phenomena such as weak knees and/or shaking hands. If none of these symptoms are evident, then this could lead to excessive reactions (breaking laws regarding self-defense) or to a breakdown in self-defense capabilities.

On top of this there are legal restrictions which only allow the use of "reasonable force" in response to an attack. In retrospect, it is easy to make such an evaluation as an outsider looking on from a comfortable armchair. Such rules (naively) require an exact evaluation of the situation which, due to the above-mentioned reasons, is often very difficult when you are caught in the middle of it. This, in the opinion of the authors, means that the "maximum response" to a self-defense situation should be trained but with variation in intensity achieved by omitting single elements from the sequence of action. In other words: it is much easier to come down from a "maximum response" to an appropriate solution than vice-versa. The optimal solution is that which allows the defender to appropriately control the situation within the limits of the law.

FIGURE 1

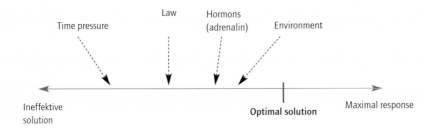

3.2 The Absorption of Strikes and Kicks in Self-defense

Through normal training in the dojang, students often get the illusion that they can avoid any strike from an attacker by using the relevant block or guard. This illusion is very dangerous because in serious cases it can lead to the fact that the psychological effect of a – not necessarily hard – strike cannot be dealt with and to the breakdown in the psychological fight and the ability to defend oneself. Everyone who is interested in serious self-defense must therefore learn to be able to deal with blows and overcome their physical and psychological effects. The term **Exposition training** in this context means that a student consciously exposes himself to his partner's strikes and kicks and trains strategies to absorb them.

As certain parts of the human body cannot be adapted to the effects of being hit (eyes, larynx, scrotum, knee) it is necessary to adapt the guard. The intensity of this exercise should be agreed by the training partners. For beginners this training should concentrate on developing a feeling for dealing with light contact (light touching) whereas for advanced students the intensity should be increased to, as far as possible, simulate reality.

The following body parts are affected most in a confrontation:

- ▶▶ Shin

- ▶▶ Thigh

- ▶▶ Trunk

- ▶▶ Torso

- ▶▶ Forearms

If these body parts are systematically trained with increasing levels of contact-intensity, the result is a psychological and physical toughening which would help the person maintain the ability to act in serious situations.

To be able to reduce the effect of an opponent's strike and kicks the following strategies are recommended:

▸▸ Tensing of stomach muscles
This prevents the techniques from reaching their maximum effect.

▸▸ Exhaling
Exhaling helps to tense the inter-costal muscles and in doing so harden the whole torso.

▸▸ Spreading the impact of the technique
The so-called *"going with"* the technique reduces its power because it does not reach the intended target.

▸▸ Changing the angle of impact
The optimal power transfer takes place at an angle of 90°. If the angle is made smaller than 90° a 100% transfer of power is no longer possible.

▸▸ Timing
In the early phases of a technique it is possible to move in to the technique to prevent it from reaching full extension. This requires good anticipation and extreme determination from the defender.

3.3   The Optimization of Power Transfer

In a self-defense situation the following problems need to be solved:

▸▸ Maintaining the ability to fight under psychological and physical pressure.
▸▸ Neutralization / absorption of opponent's power transfer.
▸▸ Optimization of one's own power transfer even under unfavorable conditions.

Wile the first two problems are dealt with in other chapters, this chapter will discuss the optimisation of one's own striking and kicking power.

3.3.1   Striking/Kicking Power

According to NEWTON's second law $F = m \times a$ (F = Force, m = Mass, a = Acceleration). This equation can also be expressed as $F = m \times \frac{v}{t}$ so that $F \times t = m$.

For power transfer the following considerations can be deduced:

Because power depends on time (t), mass (m) and velocity (v), of which the mass remains constant, we have two quantities, velocity and time, which can be influenced. Therefore, in order to maximize power, velocity is maximized and time is minimized (i.e. punching and not pushing).

3.3.2 Angle of Impact

Optimal power transfer is achieved at an angle of 90°. There are exceptions to this rule which depend on certain anatomical attributes e.g. a Tallyo-Chagi with the shin to the short ribs can be directed slightly upwards to achieve a greater effect.

3.3.3 Level of Penetration

As in competition, it is not enough to simply strike the surface of a target. To achieve an effect, it is necessary to *hit through the target or to put the focus of a strike/kick into the target.*

3.3.4 Use of the whole Body

Every technique should be executed using the whole body i.e. the **muscle chain** which makes pushing off with the ball of the foot, extending the leg, torso rotation, moving the shoulders and extending the arm possible should always be completely active.

As these optimal conditions are not always possible in self-defense, development of striking/kicking power must also be trained under unfavorable conditions (kneeling, from the ground, limited space).

3.3.5 Correct Distance

Every technique has an *ideal distance* i.e. a distance at which its optimal effect can be achieved. Due to the fact that every person is anthropologically different from the next, it is extremely important that each student finds his own ideal distance for a certain technique. As it cannot be expected that a self-defense situation offers ideal conditions, a *long and close distance version* of every technique must be trained.

3.3.6 Economical Execution

The *speed* factor in the execution of a technique is among other things influenced by the correct path to the target and by the ability to relax any muscles not used in the technique. The contraction of these muscles during a movement hinders the technique even if there is a feeling of having gained more power.

3.4 Psychological Training for Self-defense

In self-defense the psychological make-up and attitude of a person takes on a much greater significance than in competition. The best self-defense technique is useless if it is not carried out with determination and the absolute will to come out on top. In the authors' opinion, successful self-defense relies 90% on the mind and only 10% on technique!

In spite of this enormous importance, only a few aspects of psychological training will be highlighted here, as the complexity of the subject would require a whole book to discuss.

The main aim of psychologically-oriented training methods is to be able to *maintain both the psychological ability to fight and the will to come out on top.* Experience of self-defense courses shows that, regarding one's own ability to deal with a confrontation, an illusionary wishful-thinking is often common along the lines of "In training I was paralyzed by a sudden attack but in reality it will work!"

It is extremely dangerous to rely on such comforting conclusions. The probability, especially in a self-defense situation, of becoming incapable of acting due to the adrenalin rush, the unfamiliar environment and extreme stress is much more likely than the other way round.

The *self-perception of the defender* must be of such a nature that he sees himself as a potentially dangerous person. In the dojang, i.e. in a comfortable environment, it is no use being a "world champion in training" if this can not be maintained under street conditions. Overstated, this means having the perception of a predator and not of a victim.

The defender must concentrate on his strengths and not on his weaknesses. This also involves not seeing oneself as "master of 1000 holds" but rather limiting oneself to a handful of multi-functional techniques which can be adapted to almost any situation.

Under these conditions the attacker no longer represents a hostile system with certain attributes (reach, aggressiveness, weapons etc.)! He is depersonalized. Speculation about how he came to be like this and the reason for his hostility may, from a humane point of view, be very commendable but it does not contribute to resolving the situation and is therefore counterproductive.

Anyone who feels the need to legitimize the use of violence in threatening situations should realize that he is dealing with a criminal who does not respect the rules of civilized social interaction and aims to consciously terrorize or cause harm.

After these initial considerations we now come to the things that everyone interested in realistic self-defense should have clear in their minds *before* a serious confrontation. The defender must *set his own boundaries* i.e. it must be clear to him what kind of this he is prepared to ignore and at what point he will take action. Also what are his *distance thresholds*? From what distance is it possible to strike or kick first and at what distance is it too late? One further point the *degree of determination* he will use to defend himself (*killer instinct*). It can not emphasized enough that these questions must have been answered beforehand because in a self-defense situation there is no time to think about it!

An important part of this *mental preparation* is also the *visualization of threatening situations*. This can happen from the perspective of an uninvolved third party where one sees oneself reacting in a self-defense situation and experiences himself acting in the situation and actually being *successful*.

Typical intentions (e.g. "I'm controlling the situation" etc.) and *trigger phrases or trigger words* which act as a trigger for one's own actions should be integrated into training. These triggers can be interpreted as a steering mechanism as well as a kind of self-command system.

Realistic training (with protective equipment, if required) allows one to put the previously mentioned steps into practice. Suitable methods are:

▸▸ Training in every day clothing

▸▸ Training in conditions with limited visibility

▸▸ Training on different surfaces

▸▸ Training under time pressure
  • Lining up in a circle, defender stands in the center
  • Lining up in a row with attacks coming quickly one after the other

▸▸ Training the single opportunity i.e. the defender has only one chance to hit the target with his counter

For the inclusion of the pre-fight phase it is recommended to incorporate *role plays* in to training. Included in this, on the part of the attacker, are verbal manoeuvres such as insults, using language in order to distract etc.. The defender speaks in a deescalating manner becomes loud and resolute. Trigger words and technique are trained together. Facial expressions and gestures which disguise the readiness to take immediate action should be seen as important components of training so that preparation for serious confrontation can be made as realistic and effective as possible.

3.5   The five Distances of Self-defense

Every real fight can – but does not have to! – take place over the following five distances. Because of the shortness of the average self-defense conflict (less than 10 seconds) the actions of the parties take place over 1-3 of these distances. The concept of distance, however, provides great assistance in evaluating the strengths and weaknesses of a martial art and of an individual. With this there is the possibility to prevent a certain routine and to systematically compensate certain weaknesses. These five distances are as follows:

NEuTRAL DisTANCE

None of the opponents is in a position to hit the other one with a technique. This is where mostly psychological methods come into play (facial expressions, body language, use of the voice, deescalating behavior). On the part of the attacker this is where, before the actual attack, the "build up" (systematic build up of adrenalin) takes place. It is also possible that this stage is missed out!

Kicking Distance

Kicks can be executed without preparation. Discreet positioning and heightened observation on the part of the defender are necessary in order not to be caught cold.

Striking Distance

Straight punches and swinging blows are the preferred methods of attack from this distance. The defender must be prepared, depending on the action, to directly shorten or lengthen the distance.

Close Distance

At this distance, visual control of the situation is almost completely impossible. Holds, throws, knee and elbow techniques as well as hooks are executed at this distance.

Ground

Through the success of the Brazilian Jiu-Jitsu in fights where exponents of different fighting styles competed against each other, people have become aware of the importance of effective ground fighting. Even though going to ground during a confrontation is not something to aim for (especially against more than one opponent) one should look at the basic principles of ground fighting as it is an integral part of one's complete fighting ability. Let us take a look at some of the martial arts practiced in Germany and there strengths in self-defense:

Table 2

Martial Art/Distance	Neutral distance	Kicking distance	Striking distance	Close distance	Groundwork
Taekwondo	–	+ +	+	–	–
Karate	–	+ +	+	+	–
Judo	–	–	–	+ + +	+ + +
Aikido	–	+	+ +	+	+
Jiu-Jitsu	–	+	+ +	+ +	(+ +) +
Muay Thai	–	+ + +	+ +	+ + +	–
Wing Tsun	+ + +	+	+ +	+ + +	+
Wrestling	–	–	–	+ + +	+ +
Boxing	–	–	+ + +	+ +	–
Kickboxing	–	+ + +	+ + +	+	–

This matrix has no claim to objective validity but reflects the personal opinion of the authors. Therefore apologies in advance to anyone who feels offended by this and who would like to see a cross in other categories. This matrix shows, despite any subjectivity, tendencies which should be considered regarding effective self-defense.

The sportification of Taekwondo, with regard to self-defense, has mainly led to a reduction in techniques and close distance techniques in general. Most Taekwondoka, apart from those who along with Taekwondo have studied Judo or another martial art with elements of ground fighting, have not learned to fight on the ground.

Because of the deficiencies of the martial art of Taekwondo in the form practiced nowadays in most dojangs it is necessary for any Taekwondoka seriously interested in realistic self-defense to supplement his Taekwondo with foreign elements from other Budo arts. But are these elements really so foreign to today's Taekwondo as it may appear? A look the 1969 edition of General Choi's book shows that elements such as throws and locks are included! The development of Taekwondo since the formation of the WTF in 1973 to an Olympic sport in 2000 has, however, pushed these techniques into the background or banished them to oblivion.

The recommendation to complete one's Taekwondo with elements of other Budo arts is therefore nothing other than remembering the roots of Taekwondo as a martial art and starting to train the complete system. Other Budo arts are not included in their entirety. This would be impossible even if only for reasons of time. But the selection of techniques introduced in this book supplement one's own repertoire of Taekwondo techniques in a sensible way and help make self-defense more realistic and holistic!

3.6 The Position of the Defender in Relation to the Attacker

The traditional classification of attacking areas (**Olgul, Momdong, Arae**) is not sufficient for self-defense. *From the point of view of the defender* it is recommended to divide to body of the attacker into vertical zones in order to get a mental model of the advantages and disadvantages of positions in relation to the attacker.

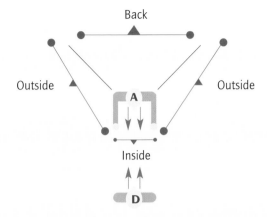

Figure 2
*Birds' eye view of attacker
(A) and defender (D)*

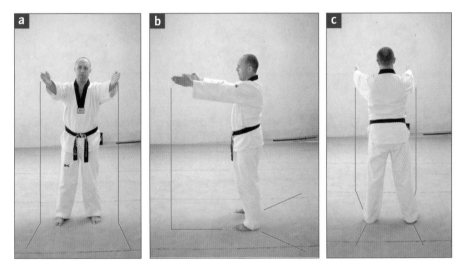

Picture 1a-c

The defender should, in serious cases, try to take a position on the outside or – optimally – behind the attacker. From here the attacker

▸▸ can easily be controlled.
▸▸ is limited in what he can do.

If the defender stands on the outside-right the attacker can no longer use or has only restricted use of the left arm and leg. Apart from this the defender finds himself outside of the field of vision which limits perception of any counter-attack. The position behind the attacker offers the advantage that sensitive parts of his body can be attacked (back of the head, neck, spine, groin, knee, Achilles tendon) without him noticing.

A block on the attacker's inside is problematic because the defender finds himself within reach of all four extremities and – depending on distance – finds himself also open to head-butts. A block on the inside should always be accompanied by a *simultaneous counter-attack* to disrupt any attack in its starting phases. If possible, the defender should move to the outside or take up a position behind the attacker.

3.7 Tactics in the vertical Zones

Each of the previously mentioned vertical zones requires a separate kind of tactical behavior because of the level of the potential threat posed in each of the areas.

▶▶ The most dangerous vertical zone for the defender is the inside because the defender finds himself within reach of all of his opponent's attacking tools (arms, legs, head). Correct tactical behavior requires that the *block and counter-attack are executed simultaneously* in order to prevent the attacker from a trying to mount a further attack. If the counter-attack is executed after the block, then the attacker can easily hit the defender. Through taking appropriate measures the defender should get to the outside of the attacker as quickly as possible.

Picture 2a-f

▸▸ If the defender succeeds in getting to the outside, the attacker will find it very difficult to the opposite side of his body. The aim of such an action is a positioning at an angle of 45-90° to the line of attack. A further advantage in getting in such a position is that the defender is on the edge or even outside of the attacker's peripheral vision which makes defense against his counter-attacks difficult to impossible.

PICTURE 3a-f

PICTURE 3g: *After throwing the opponent, his left arm is controlled with the left knee of the defender.*

PICTURE 3h-i

PICTURE 4a: *First contact (defense on the inside).*
PICTURE 4b: *Scooping movement => in doing so position on the outside.*
PICTURE 4c: *Control of the outside of the elbow.*
PICTURE 4d: *Combined elbow-neck control.*
PICTURE 4e: *Locking technique with knee.*

▸▸ If the defender manages to get behind the attacker, the opponent no longer has visual control of the situation. One danger posed to the defender in this situation is through the attacker wildly lashing out with hands or feet. One hand therefore controls and disturbs while the other strikes. Preferred targets in this situation are the back of the head, the neck, the spine, the kidneys, the groin and the knee.

In is principally true for all zones that several levels are attacked either one after another or simultaneously.

Every impulse on one level creates gaps on another.

For self-defense it is important to know the natural protective reflexes that humans have, to be able to anticipate and to uncompromisingly exploit them!

3.8 Particular Stances and Positions of the Attacker

In a Taekwondo competition the two opponents stand opposite one another. If the opponent falls or is lying on the ground it is normal practice that the other opponent does not continue kicking or striking.

In contrast to this in self-defense in order to solve the situation one must exploit the opportunities presented by a fallen opponent.

In self-defense the defender will be confronted with positions and/or body postures of the attacker, which are not common in regular Taekwondo training and therefore must be treated with extra care.

3.8.1 Crouching, Bending

This is the kind of posture, taken by wrestlers, Judoka and rugby players. The appropriate tactic consists of evading out of the direct line of attack into the outer-side and from there starting the counter-attack.

Picture 5a
Picture 5b: *Lateral moving out of the fighting line whilst controlling distance.*

PICTURE 5c-e
Note: Do not be tempted, because of a crouching opponent, to move out of the line of attack since wrestlers in particular are trained in grabbing the leg to bring their opponents to ground.

3.8.2 Kneeling

After making a mistake or stumbling it can happen that the attacker finds himself in a kneeling position:

▶▶ On one knee.

PICTURE 6a: *Shin block against a left low kick attack.*
PICTURE 6b: *Combined elbow-neck control.*
PICTURE 6c: *Interfering with the balance by using inward foot sweep.*

PICTURE 6d-g

▸▸ On both knees.

▸▸ In sitting position supported by hands.

PICTURE 7a-d
PICTURE 7e: *The left knee of the defender controls the supporting arm of the attacker to prevent a further attack.*

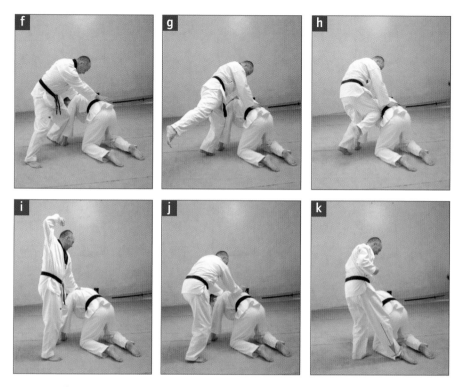

PICTURE 7f-j
PICTURE 7k: *Stamping kick to the ankle/Achilles tendon of the attacker.*

It is necessary for the defender to maintain control of the situation as, from this position, it could still be possible for the attacker to attack the groin.

3.8.3 ATTACKER HAS GONE TO GROUND

Here we differentiate between the following situations:

▸▸ lying on side.
  • facing the defender.
  • back to the defender.

a

b

c

d

e

f

g

h

Picture 8a-d
Picture 8e: *Control with the knee, the right side of the opponent's body is secured.*
Picture 8f-h

▸▸ Lying on back.

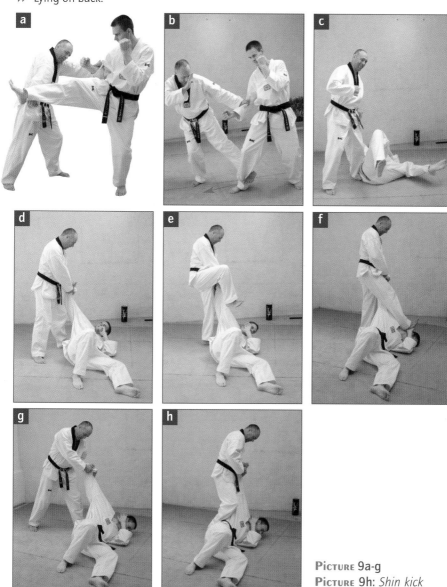

PICTURE 9a-g
PICTURE 9h: *Shin kick to the kidneys.*

▸▸ Lying on stomach.

Picture 10a
Picture 10b: *Opponent is brought down with the right leg.*
Picture 10c: *Control using forearm bar to shoulder and own body weight.*
Picture 10d: *Elbow strike to back of head.*
Picture 10e
Picture 10f: *Double open-hand strike to the back of the head.*
Picture 10g: *Regaining grip after open-hand strike, lifting head and striking it against ground.*

If the opponent is lying on the ground, the defender can and must use his knees to control and hold the opponent and to prevent any further strikes from the attacker. If possible, the "diagonal arm" (see chapter "Self-defense from the Ground") is to be used to secure the opponent on the ground. In this control situation confrontation-deciding strikes and kicks are used.

PICTURE 11a: *Double control using knees and diagonal arm.*
PICTURE 11b: *Variation of the diagonal arm.*
PICTURE 11c

3.9   The different Phases of a Confrontation

The phase concept represents – just as the concept of fighting distances – a structural aid to instructors and students, with whose help actions can be analyzed and checked regarding completeness, effectiveness and feasibility. While with the distance concept the spatial parameters are of central importance, the phase concept refers to the sequence of events of a self-defense confrontation. It is not the case that every self-defense situation must go through all phases because sometimes phases are skipped or overlap. In training, however, importance should be placed on going through *all* phases, in order to gain a sensible pattern of reaction and to fix it into the subconscious. These phases are as follows:

Pre-fight Phase

In this phase the voice, facial expressions as well as posture come into play on both the part of the attacker and the defender. If this phase is not skipped by the attacker then the defender has the possibility of deescalating the situation using the above-mentioned of means. *Role plays* should be used as an integral part of self-defense (especially in self-defense for women!). Training should be especially focused on *correct timing* for actions and on getting a feeling for when the attacker crosses over the *personal distance threshold*. Here, it should be pointed out that it is in the interest of a martial artist to determine points such as the correct timing of a self-defense confrontation, personal distance thresholds as well as the corresponding uncompromising determination of his counter-attacks and where possible to mentally go through these over and over. This must be done *before* a confrontation occurs, otherwise even the best technique will not work if, through the degree of danger in a situation or through being caught by surprise, it leads to the blocking of self-defense pattern learned in training. Certain constellations must immediately act as *triggers* i.e. trigger one's own actions, in order not to be simply rolled over. In self-defense the psychological coping mechanisms have a much higher significance than in competition, since the situation is more complex, much clear, more uncertain and, on the whole, the stakes are higher.

Initial Contact Phase

The result of this phase is either the (attempted) establishment of contact by the attacker through strikes, kicks and/or holds or the (preventive) controlling techniques of the defender.

These two phases mostly flow into one another. The controlling technique/blocks of the defender should be linked to

The Positioning Phase

Positioning in this context means that the defender lands at the edge of the attacker's field of vision i.e. to the side or at the back of the attacker, by using stepping or other methods. This is followed by the

Control Phase

in which the actual self-defense techniques (strikes, kicks, throws, holds etc) come into play. The aim of this phase is to prepare for the

End Phase

The intention of this phase is either the *incapacitation of the attacker* through neutralization (e.g. by locks, controlling holds), K. O. or – in the worst case – injury or death or the *possibility to run away* (clearly the better alternative especially for legal reasons!).

Ideally, all five phases will be looked at in self-defense training (!). For methodical reasons it will often be necessary to concentrate on a section of the entire chain in order not to push students too hard and to emphasize certain points. But this structure must always be seen as incomplete and the student must not forget the importance of the complete chain. If self-defense training is considered using the phase concept, it becomes apparent that a confrontation is ended mostly after the control phase without the end phase following on or that one puts oneself in extreme danger because the initial contact phase and positioning were not carried out exactly. One further point of criticism concerns the transfer of competition techniques into a self-defense situation, which is not very effective without in some way modifying the techniques.

4   PRIMARY ANd SECONdARY TARGETS

Primary targets are the parts of the body which when attacked cause K.O., injury or death (examples: temple, larynx, scrotum). Striking one of these targets will usually end the fight. Directly targeting these zones is however made more difficult by the fact that people have protective reflexes which are called into action whenever danger is present. *Distracting* the attacker's attention, however, makes it possible to get around these protective reflexes. This distraction can be achieved by going for so called *secondary targets*. Striking these targets will not end the fight but will cause pain and distracts attention away from primary targets, which can then be hit without the activating the protective reflexes.

Primary targets should be attacked first and foremost, in a dangerous situation, where no alternative solution can be found. Secondary targets are only attacked if access to primary targets is not directly possible and so an opening first must be created.

Primary Targets

HEAd

1. Eyes

2. Adam's apple

PICTURE 12   **PICTURE** 13

3. Nose

PICTURE 14

4. Ear

PICTURE 15: *If the ears are grabbed, they are twisted in opposite directions.*

ARM:

5. Elbow

PICTURE 16a

PICTURE 16b: *Pulling and extending the arm.*

6. Finger/back of hand

PICTURE 17a-b

PICTURE 18

PICTURE 18b: *Striking back of hand using middle knuckle fist.*

TORSO:

7. Solar plexus   8. Liver

PICTURE 19   PICTURE 20a   PICTURE 20b: *Hook to the liver.*

PICTURE 20c: *The opponent is grabbed and controlled.*   PICTURE 20d: *Knee kick to the liver.*

9. Kidneys

PICTURE 21a-b
PICTURE 21c: *Hammer fist into the kidney...*
PICTURE 21d: *... directly followed by an elbow strike.*

GROIN:

10. Scrotum

PICTURE 22a-c

PICTURE 23a: *Diagonal step out of direct line of fighting.*
PICTURE 23b: *Stamping kick to the knee joint.*
PICTURE 23c: *Interfering with opponent's balance.*
PICTURE 23d: *Conclusion using shin kick to the scrotum.*

LEG:

11. Knee

PICTURE 24a-b

PICTURE 25: *Combined defense using stopping kick to the knee and simultaneous finger strike to the eyes.*

12. Ankle/Achilles tendon

PICTURE 26a: *Inward foot sweep.*
PICTURE 26b
PICTURE 26c: *Stamping kick to the ankle/Achilles tendon.*

If the attacker is hurt, the defender should continue to consistently attack the injury!

Secondary Targets

1. Toes/instep

PICTURE 27a-c

2. Shin

PICTURE 28a-c

3. Inside thigh

PICTURE 29a-c

PICTURE **30a:** *Hook kick to inside of the opponent's thigh.*
PICTURE **30b:** *Heel of the kicking leg is pointed between legs of opponent.*
PICTURE **30c:** *Raising kicking foot to the groin area of attacker.*

4. Flanks

PICTURE 31a: *Block to side of opponent.*
PICTURE 31b: *Drawing back movement.*
PICTURE 31c: *Hammer fist to ribs.*
PICTURE 31d: *Loading and controlling the opponent on the floor.*
PICTURE 31e
PICTURE 31f: *Elbow strike into the ribs.*

5. Elbow joint

Picture 32a
Picture 32b: *Through strike to elbow opponent overextends.*
Picture 32c: *In this overextension a hook to the kidney.*

6. Shoulders

Picture 33a: *The strike to the shoulder clears the way for the decisive hook to the head.*
Picture 33b-c

The most important difference between primary and secondary targets is that strike to these targets only create gaps for more decisive blows.

5 The Subdivision of Self-defense Elements according to their Function

The elements for the optimal solution to a self-defense situation are not all of equal importance, they fulfill different functions. A subdivision of self-defense elements according to their function does not come from an extreme love of theories on the part of the authors, but serves to give more clarity to the dependency of individual actions *on each other* (sequence of events) as well as the *interdependency of actions* (simultaneous occurrence). If one defines the incapability of the attacker to continue the fight as the goal of a self-defense (e.g. by locks, holds), K.O. or injury, then the techniques which make this goal finally possible, are *main functions* (MF). Examples are: Kick to the groin, hold on the floor, elbow to the temple etc.. Techniques which clear the way for a decisive technique (disturbance of the balance, application of pain, deception, outwitting, release from the attacker) and which themselves, however, have *no decisive effect*, are techniques with *supporting functions* (SF). As well as these, there are also *self-defense elements of a non-technical nature* which fulfill *secondary functions* (2F) (Kihap, facial expression, posture, appearing self-confident, disguising the ability to defend oneself by acting incapable etc.). This subdivision helps to structure one's own self-defense chain of action. In this way it becomes clear to students *why* they do something and they will recognize the weak points in their own self-defense actions.

A graphical representation could look something like this:

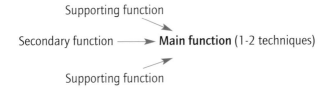

Supporting function

Secondary function ⟶ **Main function** (1-2 techniques)

Supporting function

Figure 3

Techniques with a main function are usually preceded by or are executed at the same time as 1-2 other techniques with a support function in order to achieve or increase the effect of the technique with the main function.

6 FiɡhtiNɡ DistaNce

6.1 SelecteD Examples for Self-defeNse at KickiNɡ DistaNce (= LoNɡ DistaNce, lD)

Long distance is determined by the fact that the defender can only be reached by kicking techniques. These attacks come mostly in the form of *low kicks* such as a kick to the abdomen and – as a result of *Muay Thai* – low kicks to the thigh. As a *general rule* regarding all kicks below the belt: *Never try to block with the hands*! First of all the protection of the head is sacrificed and secondly the danger of injury for hands and arms is too great! If there is no possibility to move out of the way, the best means of *blocking* is *with the shin*. Not a pleasant thought, but a kick into the abdomen, is no laughing matter either! The trick is to catch the kick *as soon as possible with the shin* which absorbs the majority of the force. By pulling the toes back, the *front shin muscle (M. tibialis anterior) is tensed* which further leads a better absorption of the kick. The calf muscle is *kept relaxed*, so that power does not work against power. To get the *shin bone used to such strain*, the following exercises are recommended:

6.1.1 BlockiNɡ aɡaiNst low Kicks

▸▸ Both partners wear shin guards.

▸▸ Only one partner wears shin guards.

▸▸ Neither partner wears shin protectors. Controlled, slow execution of low kicks. Hard execution only with agreement of both partners. Besides a physical hardening, in time, one also develops confidence in the shins as instruments of defense.

▸▸ Shin kicks into a heavy bag and arm pads.

Examples:

Low kick with front leg

▸▸ Against low outward kick.

▸▸ Against low inward kick.

PICTURE 34: *Blocking with the shin. The toes on the blocking leg point 45° outwards.*

PICTURE 35: *The block with the front shin is executed so that the toes on the blocking leg point 45° inwards.*

6.1.2 Low Kick Drills

PICTURE 36a: *The defender disturbs the balance of attacker using simultaneous attack to throat.*
PICTURE 36b

Picture 37: *At the same time as block, arm control and attack to opponent's head.*

Picture 38

Picture 39: *If the shins are not used to impact, the wearing of shin protectors is recommended.*

Picture 40

6.1.3 Examples of Transition to close Distance

Picture 41a

Picture 41b: *After defending against kick, the elbow and neck of attacker are controlled.*

Picture 41c

Picture 41d: *Through using a two-step turn, the defender is pulled into a circular movement, loses his balance and is helpless against any follow-up techniques.*

Picture 41e-f

Picture 41g: *Quickly pulling opponent to ground.*

Picture 41h-i

Picture 42a: *Opponent's kick is neutralized by giving way.*

Picture 42b

Picture 42c: *Control of the shoulders using hold on right shoulder. Pull and kick to groin.*

Picture 42d-e

Retreating from kicking techniques leads to the defender being over run. The aim must be to, as soon as possible, prevent further attacks!

6.2 Defense against medium-distance Attacks (MD)

This distance is defined by the fact that the attacker can reach the defender only with *straight or swinging punches.*

6.2.1 The Principles of defending against a straight Punch

▸▸ *Diverting* and *guiding* instead of collision of forces.

As a rule: The faster and stronger the straight attack, the smaller the energy required to change its path!

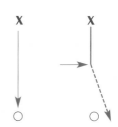

Figure 4

▸▸ Attempts to move to the *outside of the attack* and/or to the *back of the attacker.*

The use of basic techniques is unsuitable in self-defense as they are too slow. *Blocks with the palm* are used (*Batangson-Makki*), since they are fast and can easily be followed by other techniques.

Picture 43a: *Early initiation of contact with the attacking arm of the opponent.*
Picture 43b: *Diversion of attack without using much energy.*

PICTURE 44a-c

Examples of Application

PICTURE 45a: *Moving out of fighting line.*
PICTURE 45b: *Counter punch from outside.*
PICTURE 45c: *Shortening of distance using elbow strike.*
PICTURE 45d

PICTURE 46a: *Previous sequence – different angle.*
PICTURE 46b-d

PICTURE 47a
PICTURE 47b: *Opponent is easily turned by the shovel movement after the defense technique, and the defender lands on outside.*
PICTURE 47c

PICTURE 48a: *Using double block punch is diverted.*
PICTURE 48b: *Using a lock opponent is taken to ground with rotation of body.*
PICTURE 48c

PICTURE 49a
PICTURE 49b: *After diverting attacking kick, the arm on the same side must directly be controlled at the elbow to prevent further attacks.*
PICTURE 49c: *Hand claw to the eyes.*
PICTURE 49d: *Throw.*

6.2.2 The Principles of defending against a swinging Punch

Swinging punches semi-circular, mostly completely uncontrolled and wildly executed attacks which are swung along way from behind the attacker.

Through their route to the target they develop large force, during the execution, however, the attacker is open to counter-attacks. Due to the fact that the attack is swung from behind the attacker the defender automatically finds himself on the *inside*, e.g., within reach of both arms and legs. Dodging to the side is not possible apart from when done in connection with twisting movement. Moving backwards is also out of the question, since the defender can easily be over run.

▶▶ *Directly moving forward whilst maintaining guard.*

By directly moving forward the defender is in only in reach of techniques which have not obtained maximum power. If hit, the effect will be minimal.

▶▶ *Simultaneous counter-attack.*

Since the defender is in range of all extremities of the attacker, it is necessary to execute an immediate counter-attack.

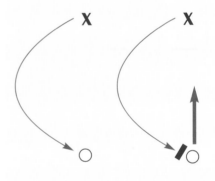

Figure 5

Examples of Application

Picture 50a: *The block is directed diagonally forwards into the semicircular attack. Followed directly by the body of the defender.*
Picture 50b: *Knife-hand strike to the neck.*
Picture 50c
Picture 50d: *Dodging sideward, neck and elbow control, turning with throw.*
Picture 50e-f

Picture 51a-k

Picture 52a: *Block with simultaneous hand claw to the eyes.*
Picture 52b: *Breaking the balance.*
Picture 52c: *Start of throw.*
Picture 52d-g

71

PICTURE 53a-b
PICTURE 53c: *Eye squeezing.*
PICTURE 53d: *Head butt.*
PICTURE 53e-g

6.3   Close Distance (CD)

Most self-defense takes place in the close distance, which reflects in the *number* and *variety* of possible attacks. Regardless of the significance of mastering self-defense solutions for this distance, conventional Taekwondo training prepares students least for the requirements at this distance. Due to the emphasis of many schools on sport Taekwondo, students are taught not to use many protective mechanisms (e.g. guarding of the head). The realistic use of the hands is not effectively trained due to the almost exclusive emphasis on leg techniques. In order to supplement the Taekwondo repertoire of technique it is worthwhile acquiring close contact training methods and techniques from related disciplines such as full contact Karate, Muay Thai, Ju-Jitsu, and Wing Tsun. In considering older Taekwondo books (I'm thinking above all again of Choi Hong Hi, Taekwondo, from 1969) one recognizes that many of these specialized techniques not used today are not at all so foreign. They have just been *banished to oblivion not trained with regard to self-defense*. Some of the more important close distance techniques include:

▸▸ Knee kicks (to the thigh, torso, head. Execution: forward, semicircular, jumping).

▸▸ Elbow strikes (semicircular-forwards, sideward, backwards, downward).

▸▸ Disturbance of balance (see book).

▸▸ Low Kicks (stopping kick, stamping kick, shin kick to the legs).

▸▸ Head butt.

▸▸ Control techniques (see book).

6.3.1   Selected Defense Techniques against close-distance Attacks

These techniques *do not* represent the only possible ways of dealing with the attacks described here. This is, however, a *range of simple, versatile techniques* with the *potential to quickly bring an end to a threatening situation*. Due to the close distance the overview of the situation is quickly lost. Therefore only techniques should be used which can be brought hard and directly to the target. *Perhaps* there will be the possibility to use locks, holds and throws but this should not be the aim! In close distance situations techniques should not be executed half-heartedly. The aim must be to end the conflict *as soon as possible (and to your own favor!)*. Since in the close distance does not allow much room for acceleration, development of maximum force over a short distance must be trained on a *heavy bag* and *arm pads*.

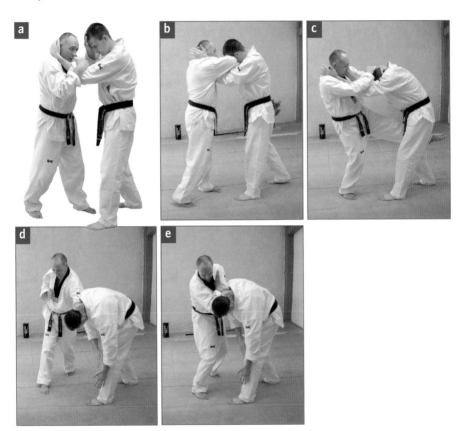

Picture 54a: *Head butt is neutralized using palm of hand.*
Picture 54b: *Elbow strike.*
Picture 54c
Picture 54d: *Dodging sideways out of fighting line.*
Picture 54e: *followed by elbow strike executed diagonally upwards.*

Picture 55a

Picture 55b: *The right hand hooks under the attacking elbow.*

Picture 55c: *Continuation of the attack.*

Picture 55d: *The left hand retakes control of the elbow.*

Picture 55e

Picture 56a: *The elbow of the opponent is pulled towards own right hip.*
Picture 56b: *At the same time head control with the left hand.*
Picture 56c: *Beginning of two-step turn.*
Picture 56d
Picture 56e: *Head control with the knee/knee kick.*
Picture 56f

Picture 57a: *Choking the opponent from the front, control and securing of the right wrist with simultaneous finger strike to the eye.*

Picture 57b: *Turning away from line of attack.*

Picture 57c: *Extension of diagonal right arm – left leg using stopping kick to inside of left knee of opponent. In doing so the arm to be attacked is extended, and the lock can be carried out.*

Picture 57d: *Disturbance of the balance using lock with the shoulder/upper arm.*

Picture 57e: *Execution of extending lock.*

Picture 57f: *Securing to ground using knee.*

Picture 58a: *Choke hold from the side. Protection of the neck by shrugging shoulders and taking control of opponent's left hand.*

Picture 58b: *Knife-hand strike to the short ribs causes shock.*

Picture 58c: *Hold is put on.*

Picture 58d-f

PICTURE 59a: *Protection of the neck shrugging shoulders. At the same time the arms are tensed, rotated inward and brought forward.*

PICTURE 59b: *Dodging back to the left while turning clockwise.*

PICTURE 59c: *Lock.*

PICTURE 59d

PICTURE 59e: *Extending arm of opponent.*

PICTURE 59f-g

6.4   Self-defense from the Ground

For Taekwondoka who practice their martial art standing up, self-defense on the ground presents a particular challenge, since they are not able to use the majority of techniques they have learned or they must adapt their techniques to the situation. Currently the focus of the interest within martial arts is directed considerably towards *grappling*. This interest was aroused particularly by the success of the Brazilian Jiu Jitsu in competitions of different styles in *Cage Fights*, *Ultimate Fights* etc.. The impression developed – and it was also greatly supported by commercial marketing – that the ability to fight on the ground makes a martial artist almost "invincible". It is correct to say that ability on the ground and the knowledge of what to do in a serious situation helps to round off one's self-defense capabilities but this should not lead to an over-exaggeration of the ground as a fighting distance. Going to ground in order to successfully end a self-defense situation is sometimes recommended it. The following facts contradict this:

▸▸ In a ground fighting situation I am, to a large extent, *immobile*. The sudden appearance of further opponents will certainly lead to my defeat.
▸▸ *Limited vision* while fighting on the ground. Most of the time I can not see if another opponent tries to intervene.
▸▸ Ground fighting is *energy sapping*. The best option is to *get back on one's feet as quickly is possible*.

On the other side of the spectrum there are those who are convinced that if they do not want to go to ground, no one can put them down and therefore they see no reason to train ground fighting. This attitude shows a kind of ignorance and greatly removed from reality. Any Taekwondoka interested in serious self-defense will take time to look at this "foreign" area. If possible, it is very helpful to *spend some time studying judo* (good supplement also because of the *falling* and *throwing*!). The consideration is always in the mind of how I can *integrate* techniques from Taekwondo *into the ground fighting*. In contrast to judo aim is not to force the opponent to give up by using holds, choke holds or locks but to see these as a way to get into a position to be able to use kicks and punches, in order to get to one's feet as quickly as possible.

After looking at the role ground fighting plays in self-defense let us now consider some techniques and principles used in ground fighting:

▸▸ Attacker in standing position, defender on the ground.
▸▸ Attacker and defender are both on the ground.

The idea behind the first constellation is, while in an unfavorable position, the ability to:

1. to keep the attacker away and
2. while considering personal safety, getting to a standing position.

Let us now take a look at the most favorable position to take whilst on the ground. The *geometric figure*, which offers the smallest surface area to an attacker, is the *ball*. The hands are in *defensive position*, in order to be able to strike or grab. The body lies half on the side, head and shoulders are raised (!). This requires strong torso muscles! Both legs bent and tucked in to the body. The *lower leg protects the abdomen*, while the *upper is bent and ready to kick*. Kicking targets are the shin, knee and abdomen of the attacker.

PICTURE 60: *The position of the defender approximates that of a ball. The upper leg is tucked in ready to kick, the lower leg is folded into the lower body, in order to protect the groin. The hands are raised ready to grab -, defend and strike.*

PICTURE 61: *Kick to knee.*   **PICTURE 62:** *Kick to groin.*   **PICTURE 63:** *Locking the leg by hooking the ankle and simultaneously kicking to knee.*

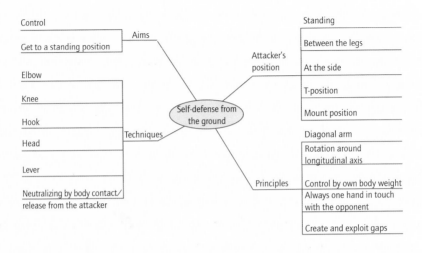

Control		Aims			Standing

Control

Get to a standing position — Aims

Elbow

Knee

Hook — Techniques

Head

Lever

Neutralizing by body contact/
release from the attacker

Self-defense from the ground

Attacker's position — Standing

Between the legs

At the side

T-position

Mount position

Principles — Diagonal arm

Rotation around longitudinal axis

Control by own body weight
Always one hand in touch with the opponent

Create and exploit gaps

MindMap1: *Self-defense from the ground*

6.4.1 Training Exercises

▸▸ The attacker tries to *get past the feet of the defender* in order to control him. The defender stays ready and turns so that his feet are always between himself and the attacker.

▸▸ The attacker is standing at the side of the defender who is lying on the ground. The defender brings his *legs between himself and the attacker* (protective equipment for legs and abdomen!).

Picture 64a-b
Picture 64c: *Pull back for knee kick.*
Picture 64d: *The attacker is turned by the knee kick.*
Picture 64e: *The defender controls the attacker using a leg lock.*

▸▸ *Pad training* with large pad for kicks from the ground (heel kicks, side kicks). Developing optimal force for these kicks is bio mechanically not possible, due to the fact that factors such as the reaction of the shoulders, the optimal use of the hip etc. are not present. Despite these handicaps the maximum possible kicking power should be generated.

▸▸ *Standing up and moving away from the opponent.* After being kicked or the retreat of the attacker standing up and moving away from opponent. The attacker tries to prevent this.

PICTURE 65a
PICTURE 65b: *Rising to feet away from the opponent.*
PICTURE 65c-d

The second constellation (attacker and defender both on the ground) there are the following *basic positions of the attacker in relation to the defender:*

a) The attacker finds himself between the legs of the defender.

b) The attacker finds himself at the side of the defender.

PICTURE 66

PICTURE 67

c) The attacker lies laterally on the defender.

d) The attacker is above the head of the defender.

PICTURE 68

PICTURE 69

e) The attacker sits, is kneeling on the defender (stomach side!).

Picture 70a-b

f) The attacker sits, is kneeling on the back of the lying defender.

Picture 71

The defender should train so that he is able to use kicks, strikes, locks etc. from the following positions:

- Side-on position to the attacker.
- At least one knee between defender and attacker.
- Hands covering space between attacker and defender (a hand is used to control, the other strikes others, pokes, tears, squeezes).

6.4.2 Additional technical Elements for Defense from the Ground

▸▸ Turning/rolling the attacker using legs.

Picture 72a

Picture 72b: *Hanging foot on inside of left thigh of the opponent.*

Picture 72c: *The left hand of defender initiates contact whilst simultaneously pulling neck.*

Picture 72d: *Rolling over attacker with a sharp pull of the head towards left side of body and raising of the hooked right leg.*

Picture 72e-f

▸▸ Position of the diagonal arm of the attacker.

Picture 73a
Picture 73b: *Divert the right arm to the diagonal arm.*
Picture 73c: *Grab to the eyes.*
Picture 73d: *Rolling the opponent over.*
Picture 73e

6.4.3 Examples

We have consciously kept the demonstrated self-defense sequences quite general, as the is that many of the theoretically described principles can be put into practice.

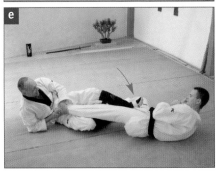

PICTURE 74a: *Block with hands and shin against attempted kick.*
PICTURE 74b: *Seizing the leg. Lock using own left foot. At the same time blocking the support leg with the right foot.*
PICTURE 74c
PICTURE 74d: *Pulling back for heel kick.*
PICTURE 74e: *Heel kick to groin.*
PICTURE 74f

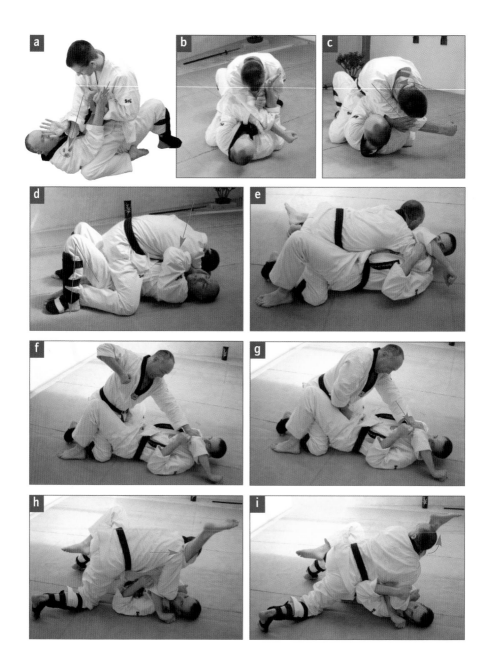

PICTURE 75a: *Diverting attempted strike to the diagonal arm while simultaneously blocking the left striking hand.*
PICTURE 75b: *Diagonal arm.*
PICTURE 75c: *Neck pull.*
PICTURE 75d: *Pulling down the opponent and securing him to own body while blocking the right leg with left foot.*
PICTURE 75e: *Rolling opponent over.*

PICTURE 75f: *Block the opposing arm.*
PICTURE 75g: *Punch to the groin.*
PICTURE 75h: *Escaped from between the legs of the opponent.*
PICTURE 75i: *Moving closely around the raised leg.*
PICTURE 75j: *The opponents arm is fixed diagonally around the neck.*
PICTURE 75k: *Strike to the face.*
PICTURE 75l: *Followed by elbow strike.*
PICTURE 75m: *Seize the head. Pulling back for knee kick.*
PICTURE 75n: *Knee kick to the head of the opponent from the lying position.*

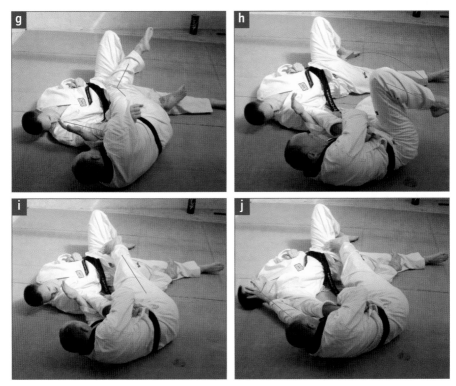

PICTURE **76a:** *Worst conceivable situation: Opponent sits on the back and chokes the defender.*

PICTURE **76b:** *Strategy: Become small. Head is pulled between the shoulders. Hip moves upwards. Knees and elbow are as far as possible held to one side.*

PICTURE **76c:** *This "fence" is used as lever, in order to explosively throw the opponent off the back. Own body accompanies the turn.*

PICTURE **76d:** *Defender falls onto the attacker and strikes directly with a right hook to the face of the attacker.*

PICTURE **76e:** *The left leg of the defender secures the left leg of the attacker by hanging into it. Simultaneous use of lock.*

PICTURE **76f:** *Pulling back for knee kick into the groin.*

PICTURE **76g:** *Execution of the knee kick.*

PICTURE **76h:** *Pulling back for roundhouse kick.*

PICTURE **76i:** *Execution of kick.*

PICTURE **76j:** *Finger stab to the eyes.*

PICTURE 77a: *Choke hold kneeling at the side of the defender. The shoulder is pulled up to protect the neck.*

PICTURE 77b: *Finger stab to the eye.*

PICTURE 77c: *Breaking the balance.*

PICTURE 77d: *Turning around: the left hand seizes right ear of the attacker, turning and tearing. Simultaneously the right hand pushes the left upper arm and/or the left shoulder of the attacker upwards.*

PICTURE 77e: *Elbow strike to the head.*

PICTURE 77f: *Knife-hand strike to the neck.*

PICTURE 77g: *Right hand seizes the neck, followed by a head butt.*

PICTURE 77h: *Kick to the ribs/kidneys.*

PICTURE 77i: *Stamping kick to the ribs and release from opponent.*

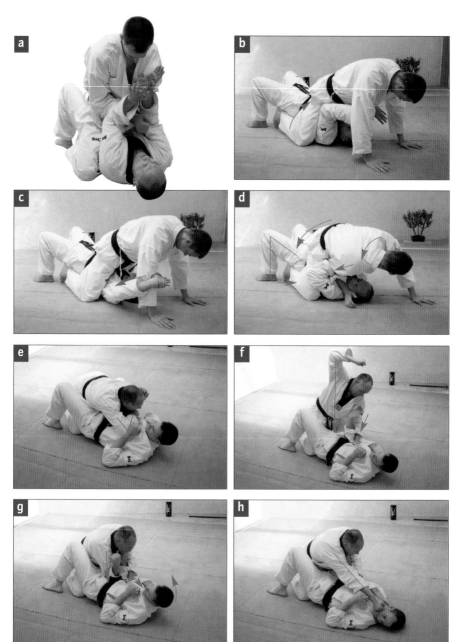

Continued on the next page

Picture 78a: *The opponent sits on the stomach of defender. Both hands of the defender are raised for protection and are ready for action.*

Picture 78b: *The balance of the attacker is disturbed by the defender explosively rearing up . The attacker is forced to support himself.*

Picture 78c: *The defender uses this to place a two handed grip on the right elbow of the attacker..*

Picture 78d: *... and jerkily pulls him towards himself. The right body side of the attacker is secured and used as rotation axis.*

Picture 78f: *After the rotation on the floor the defender secures the attacker by holding the forearm crosswise and using his body weight.*

Picture 78g: *The left hand of the defender controls the right arm of the attacker while he is drawing his right arm back for an elbow strike.*

Picture 78h: *Elbow strike to the abdomen. As a reaction to it the head of the opponent comes upward.*

Picture 78i: *The defender exploits this and strikes with a punch to the face.*

Picture 78j: *Followed by another elbow strike to the abdomen.*

Picture 78k: *In order to arrive at the open side of the attacker, the defender slips his right knee over the left inside thigh of the attacker. (Your training partner will not think very highly of you if you do not take care when doing this!)*

PICTURE 78l: *The neck of the attacker is secured with the right forearm.*

PICTURE 78m

PICTURE 78n: *Pulling back for an elbow strike.*

PICTURE 78o: *Use of body weight in elbow strike.*

PICTURE 78p: *Pulling back for the final knee kick while simultaneously securing head of the attacker.*

PICTURE 78q: *Execution of decisive knee kick.*

Continued on the next page

Picture 79a: *Attacker holds the defender down on the ground.*

Picture 79b: *The defender makes room for by rearing up...*

Picture 79c: *... into which he then slides his right knee between himself and the attacker.*

Picture 79d: *Change of angle: he presses against the neck of his opponent and secures the left knee of the attacker with his right hand.*

Picture 79e: *Right elbow strike to the ribs.*

Picture 79f: *Left elbow strike to the neck.*

Picture 79g: *Turning the attacker.*
Picture 79h: *Lock on left arm of the attacker.*
Picture 79i: *Fierce execution of technique.*

6.4.4 Selected Ground Techniques

▸▸ Fist (vertical fist, Sewo Chirugi, at short distance) e.g. to the larynx.

Picture 80: *Simultaneous diversion of the attack and counter-attack with the erected fist.*

Picture 81: *Effect of erected fist punch – here to the larynx – is greatly increased by simultaneously pulling the neck.*

▸▸ Finger poking/eye squeezing.

PICTURE 82: *At the same time as blocking of the arms with an elbow bar, eyes are attacked with fingertip strike.*

▸▸ Elbow from the ground.

PICTURE 83: *Elbow strike while pulling neck.*

▶▶ Neck hold.

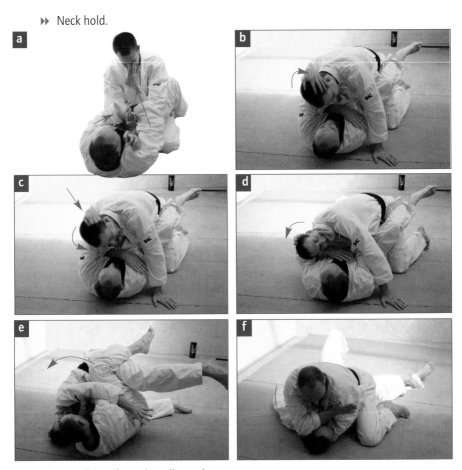

Picture 84a: *Fingertip strike to the eye.*

Picture 84b: *Initiation of contact to the head of the attacker. Careful! The right hand of the defender is positioned on the chin, the left hand is positioned around the head of the opponent.*

Picture 84c: *If the hair of the attacker is long enough, this offers the possibility for a determined pull of the hair. Careful while training! This is a potentially lethal technique, if jerked backwards this can lead to the breaking of the neck and most probably death.*

Picture 84d: *The head of the attacker is rotated.*

Picture 84e: *The defender turns with him.*

Picture 84f: *The defense sequence is completed with elbow strike to the head.*

▸▸ Knee.

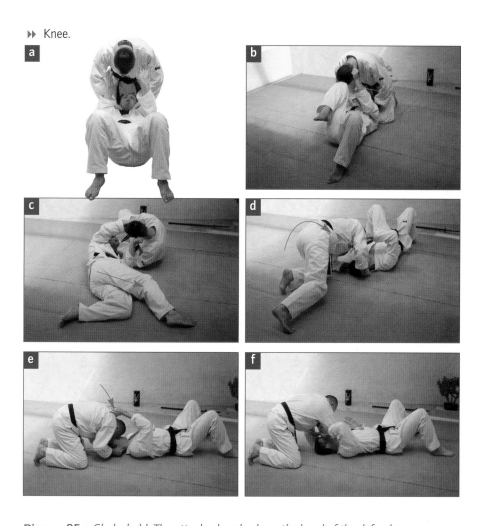

Picture 85a: *Choke hold: The attacker kneels above the head of the defender.*
Picture 85b: *Defender seizes the ears of the attacker, twists them in opposite directions and strikes with the knee to the top of the head.*
Picture 85c: *The head of the attacker is turned further in a clockwise direction. Through the twisting of the ears he has no possibility to get away.*
Picture 85d
Picture 85e: *Head butt to the face of the attacker follows.*
Picture 85f: *Final technique: Elbow strike to the face or neck.*

7 Falling

Although familiar to Judoka and Jiu Jitsuka, falling is something quite unknown to Taekwondoka. Not only does *safe falling* play a role in self-defense, but also in competition and in everyday life. Optimal falling, without hurting oneself, requires certain behaviors, which function in a different way to natural reflexes. The natural reaction to falling down is to attempt to use the hands to stop the fall. The heavier the fall, the more dangerous this kind falling becomes. *Weak points such as fingers, wrists, elbows and shoulders*, are especially affected since the whole force of the fall is concentrated on a relatively small supporting surface. The principles for safe falling are as follows:

▸▸ Distribution of the force of the fall over t*he largest possible surface area.*

▸▸ [=> break fall (slapping the ground to cushion the fall) at an angle of 45° to body, a larger angle makes the break fall ineffective!].

▸▸ Active use of the counter force of fall (*short, springy break fall*, since according to the theory of momentum F x t = m x v the greater the power, the shorter the time.).

▸▸ Do not leave any corners or edges (elbows, shoulders). The *ideal form for rolling movements is the ball*!

Falling exercises:

Role forwards, backwards.

Picture 86a-b

Laterally.

Picture 87a-c

Forwards.

Picture 88a
Picture 88b: *For stabilization while falling forwards, it is important to slightly bend the hips to prevent the middle body from hitting the floor too hard. The elbow are positioned beneath the shoulders.*

Backwards.

Picture 89a-e

The use of mats is essential to safety in the training of falling techniques (Judo mats, gymnastics mats)!

Once the falling techniques have been mastered, they can be also be practiced on a normal hall floor.

8   INTERFERING WITH BALANCE OF THE ATTACKER

If it happens in a self-defense situation that the attacker loses his balance his *natural reflex* is to try to regain tie balance. This means that the opponent is forced to think in two steps:

1. Regain balance.
2. Attack.

However, our thinking as a defender has only one step: end the conflict with a decisive blow! We therefore have a slight advantage (!) as far as time is concerned and on top of this it is possible to attack primary targets which will enable us to end the conflict (when resistance on the part of the attacker is limited).

Here are some methods for interfering with the balance of the attacker:

8.1   Pushing

Jerkily pushing head, shoulders, pelvis.

PICTURE 90a: *The balance of the attacker is disturbed by pushing towards head.*
PICTURE 90b: *This momentary helplessness of the attacker is exploited by a counter punch.*

Picture 91a: *The push at the top of the shoulders leads to an increase in distance to kicking distance.*
Picture 91b
Picture 91c: *Final kick to the stomach.*

Picture 92a: *Pushing with stop kick.*
Picture 92b: *Kick to the abdomen.*

8.2 Pulling

Elbow, pelvis as points of orientation.

Picture 93a-c

8.3 Alternating Movements

▸▸ Push – Pull/Pull – Push.

▸▸ Push – Pull – Push/Pull – Push – Pull.

Picture 94a-d

8.4 SWEEPING

▸▸ Soto Ashi Barai.

PICTURE 95a-c

PICTURE 95d: *With the outward sweep the not yet fully supporting leg is further swept towards the toes. The left hand of the defender makes a movement to the opposite direction, in order to completely disturb the balance of the attacker. The center of gravity of the defender should always be lower than that of the attacker.*

PICTURE 95e

▸▸ Uchi Ashi Barai / Ko-Uchi-Gari.

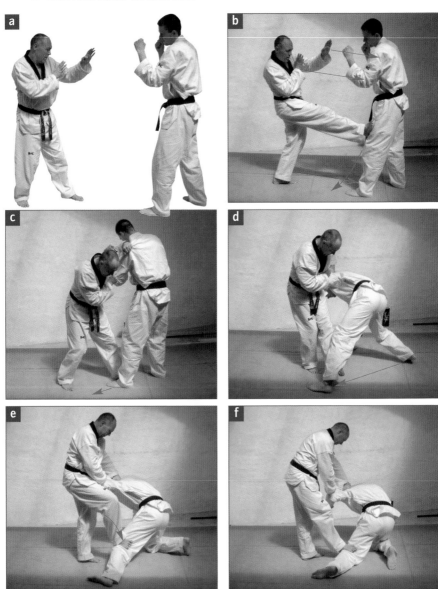

PICTURE 96a

PICTURE 96b: *The stop kick to the thigh prepares the initiation of contact at the elbow and the shoulder of the attacker.*

PICTURE 96c: *Beginning the inward sweep.*

PICTURE 96d: *Through the widening of the stance of the attacker he becomes unsteady.*

PICTURE 96e: *Sideward stamping kick to the knee of the attacker. Careful! When practicing, extreme caution is necessary, because even small forces might injure the training partner.*

PICTURE 96f-g

PICTURE 96h: *Elbow strike to the neck of the attacker.*

▸▸ O-Uchi-Gari.

PICTURE 97a: *Opponent's kick is diverted from the inside. At the same time counter-attack towards the face of the attacker.*
PICTURE 97b: *The attacker is secured.*
PICTURE 97c: *The attacker is brought down using a turning motion.*
PICTURE 97d

▸▸ O-Soto-Gari.

PICTURE 98a: *The kick attack is taken past body side of the defender.*
PICTURE 98b: *Control of elbow and head.*
PICTURE 98c: *The head of the attacker is secured to body of the defender.*
PICTURE 98d: *Throw.*
PICTURE 98e-f

8.5 Further Takedowns

The two techniques presented in the following originally come from Aikido. They can be applied in self-defense since they are very easy to learn and offer a good possibility of bringing the attacker to ground.

▶▶ Irimi-Nage.

Picture 99a
Picture 99b: *The right arm of the defender covers the head of the attacker. A controlled circular throw follows.*
Picture 99c

▸▸ Kaiten-Nage.

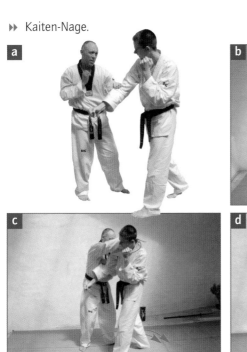

PICTURE 100a-b

PICTURE 100c: *The attacker is turned using a two-step 180° turn.*

PICTURE 100d: *Starting point for throw (= Kaiten-Nage).*

PICTURE 100e: *Throwing.*

PICTURE 100f

9   Useful Techniques for the Defender

9.1   Low Kicks

In Taekwondo much care and effort has been put into the development and perfection of high kicks. In self-defense, however, the focus is on low kicks as these can be carried out *without risk*. These low kicks *serve mostly to prepare for something else* (covering distance, stopping, distraction from other techniques) but they can also be used to *end a conflict* (e.g. stamping kick to attacker who has gone to ground).

For self-defense, a Taekwondoka should train the following supplementary low kicks:

9.1.1 Murup-chagi

Effective kick for extreme close combat. An important factor here is the upper-body control of the opponent, since any small change in distance will make this kick ineffective.

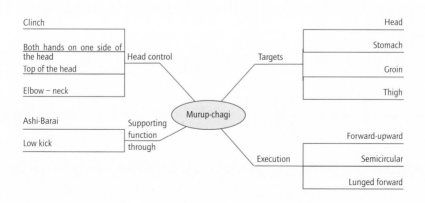

Mindmap 2: *Murup-chagi*

TARGETS

PICTURE 101: *Head.*

PICTURE 102: *Stomach.*

PICTURE 103: *Groin.*

PICTURE 104: *Interior thigh.*

Execution

Under the category "targets" the *forward-upward* execution was demonstrated. In the following the *semicircular* as well as *lunging forward uses* are shown.

PICTURE 105: *Semicircular execution.*

PICTURE 106a: *The raised knee is lunged forward using power from the hip.*
PICTURE 106b: *Particularly suitable for creating space in close-combat.*

Supporting Function through...

In order to increase the effect of the knee kick as an individual technique, techniques can be used which disturb the balance of the opponent, lengthen his reaction time, and generally put him in a state of helplessness.

PICTURE 107a: *Using the inward sweep the Λ of his legs is widened and possible targets are exposed.*
PICTURE 107b: *Kick to the groin.*

PICTURE 108a
PICTURE 108b: *The inward low kick fulfils the same function as an inward sweep, it widens the Λ of the legs of the attacker.*
PICTURE 108c-d

Head Control

See chapter 12 "Methods of Head Control".

9.1.2   Ap-chagi

In self-defense there are many targets for the front kick. The most common is a direct kick to the abdomen of the attacker, which is best prepared for using and inward sweep, inward low kick or knee kick to the thigh, in order to render protective reflexes of the opponent ineffective.

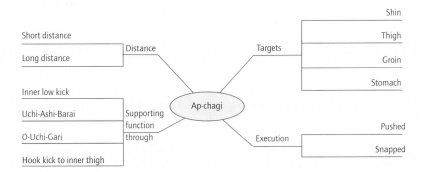

Mindmap 3: *Ap-chagi*

Targets

Picture 109: *Shin.*   **Picture 110:** *Knee/thigh.*

Picture 111: *Groin.*   **Picture 112:** *Stomach.*

Execution

There are two possible ways to execute this technique:

With the pushing variant the focus of the technique is aimed inside the opponent inside and trajectory is straight (see last picture in the section "targets"). With the snapped variation a the trajectory is semicircular and an emphasis is placed on pulling the leg back after the kick (whip principle).

Picture 113a
Picture 113b: *The length of the arrows shows that the pull back movement is much more important than the actual execution of the kick.*

Supporting Function through...

PICTURE 114a: *Inward low kick, widening the Λ.*
PICTURE 114b: *Execution of kick.*

PICTURE 115a-c

PICTURE 116a: *O-Uchi-Gari.*
PICTURE 116b

PICTURE 117a: *Hook kick to inner thigh of attacker.*
PICTURE 117b

DISTANCE

At a distance where knee kicks are not possible and which is too short for kicking techniques, effective kicks can, despite these handicaps, be brought into play if one observes the following criteria:

▸▸ The distance is artificially extended if the hip is consciously pulled in (see picture).
▸▸ The effect of the kick is increased by pulling the attacker into the kick.

For self-defense training, the authors recommend training a long and a short distance version of every technique. The short distance version may not satisfy the aesthetic needs of the Taekwondo practitioner but the probability of finding the optimal conditions for a perfect Taekwondo technique in a self-defense situation is rather small. The importance of being able to generate powerful techniques, also under unfavorable conditions (limited distance, inhibiting factors such as restrictive clothing, unstable balance etc.), cannot be emphasized enough!

Picture 118: *Short distance version of an Ap-Chagi.* **Picture 119:** *Long distance version.*

9.1.3 Low Kick/Tollyo-chagi (inward and outward)

Low Kicks are an indispensable tool for street fighting, since they can be executed very powerfully and are difficult to defend against. In training one should make sure that when executing this kick, the guard covers the head.

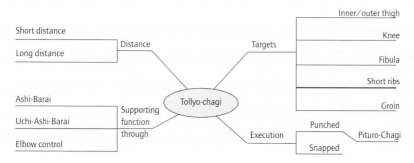

Mindmap 4: *Tollyo-chagi*

TARGETS

PICTURE 120: *Inner thigh. The kick goes diagonally upwards from the bottom to upper-outside. The aim is to disturb stable stance of the attacker and to open his Λ to subsequent attacks.*

PICTURE 121: *Outer thigh. By attacking this area, the nerves on the outside of the thigh of the attacker are hit. This can result in a temporary loss of use of the leg. The angle of impact of the kick is 90°. By pivoting hip, the kick can be easily angled downwards. This leads to a sudden stretching of attacked musculature, which causes the attacker to drop to his knees.*

Picture 122a: *Kick to fibula.*

Picture 122b: *This kick works in a similar way to an outward foot sweep. The impact of the shin can lead to a break of the fibula of the attacker, which would end the conflict.*

Picture 123: *Shin kick to the short ribs. In order to obtain maximum effect, it is recommended to slightly angle the kick upwards.*

Picture 124a: *Kick to the abdomen.*
Picture 124b: *This is a typical short distance kick. Due to the position of the torso on the out side, i.e. bending to the side whilst controlling the attacking arm from the outside, a gap is created which can be exploited by using a short, sharp kick to the lower abdomen.*

Execution

Picture 125a: *Pituro-chagi. Kicking "around the corner". This means a semi-circular kick from the inside to the outside.*
Picture 125b: *In competition Taekwondo this kick is no longer used. However, for self-defense it plays a valuable role because of the way it can take the attacker by surprise.*

Picture 126a: *Low-Section Pushing Kick. The kick can be considered a close combat technique, which is used to overextend the attacker's leg and thus disturb his balance.*

Picture 126b: *The kicking shin is brought into the starting position, parallel to the ground, and is then directly rammed diagonally downward into the thigh of the opponent.*

Picture 126c

Supporting Function through...

For illustration see the chapters of the corresponding techniques.

Distance

It is important that these techniques can be executed with power even at closer distances. The integration of close-distance exercises into training is recommended.

9.1.4 Stop Kick

Kick with the inside (toes point approx. 45° outward) or the outside edge (toes point approx. 45° inward) of the foot to the shin, knee, thigh, hip joint of the attacker. If the stop kick is executed as a traditional Yop-Chagi, there is the danger that the attacker will get behind the defender.

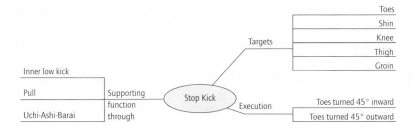

Mindmap 5: *Stop Kick*

Targets

With the versions specified here, the toes are turned approx. 45° outwards. Attacking tool is the edge/sole of the foot. These kicks are very difficult to block, since they can also be executed at a close distance. On top of this they provide an excellent starting point for subsequent techniques.

Picture 127: *Target area instep/shin.*   **Picture 128:** *Target area knee/thigh.*   **Picture 129:** *Target area groin/lower abdomen.*

EXECUTION

PICTURE 130: *With this version the toes are turned approx. 45° inward. This is a variation on the Yop-Chagi. The disadvantage of this version is that if the defender misses the target he stands exposed and the attacker can quickly get behind him.*

SUPPORTING FUNCTION THROUGH...

PICTURE 131a: *Inward low kick*
PICTURE 131b: *The stance of the opponent is unsteadied by the previous technique. The following stop kick completely knocks him off balance.*

9.1.5 STAMPING Kick

▸▸ Against an attacker lying on the ground.
▸▸ Backwards to toes/instep.
▸▸ Forwards to toes/instep.

Inside edge of the kicking foot hits the shin and continues in a downward movement through to the foot.

For illustrations see previous chapters.

9.2 Hand Techniques in Self-defense

9.2.1 Chirugi/Batangson

The value of striking techniques in self-defense is justified by their speed and hardness. In contrast to competition and basic Taekwondo, the Sewo-Chirugi (vertical-fist) punch is used.

The position of the fist provides the wrist with greater stability and therefore reduces the risk of injury in a confrontation. Striking with the palm-heel make it also possible for women with weak wrists to apply hard-impact techniques in self-defense.

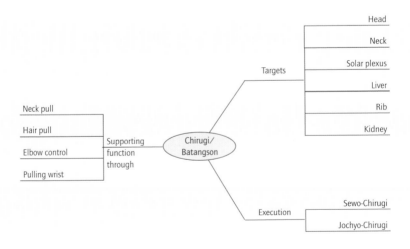

MindMap 6: Chirugi/Batangson

Picture 132a: *Starting position for a vertical-fist snap punch.*
Picture 132b
Picture 132c: *Observe the position of the fist!*

The vertical-fist can be adapted so that the knuckles always strike, at any height, without losing stability! This is not the case for a normal punch.

Picture 133: *Use of the vertical fist.*

9.2.2 Hooks

Hooks make it possible to obtain an effect from a short distance and to strike around obstacles such as the guard.

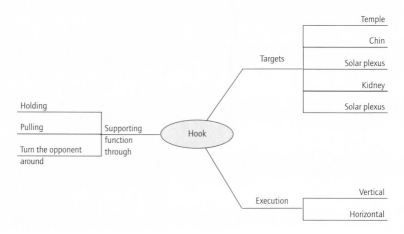

Mindmap 7: *Hooks*

Picture 134: *To increase the effect of the strike it is necessary to integrate the hip rotation and leg extension into the technique. The hip rotation is made possible by an outward rotation and raising of the heel on the side of impact.*

Picture 135a: *Because of the shoveling movement of the left arm of the defender the left side of the attacker's torso is opened up and exposed.*
Picture 135b: *A hook to the short ribs follows.*

9.2.3 Pyonsonkut-chirugi

The preferred targets for the fingertip strike are the eyes. No real power is needed for this, but precision and speed are necessary. The attacking tool is the *fingertip* [Figure 6]. Since the hand is angled towards the forearm, this prevents injury if the fingers strike a hard surface. The eyes can be attacked also with the *hand claw*.

Figure 6

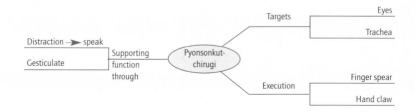

Mindmap 8: *Pyonsonkut-chirugi*

Picture 136a

Picture 136b: *The effect of the claw hand into the eyes is increased by pulling the neck. This means that the attacker cannot evade.*

Picture 137: *Considers the angle of the hand!*

Picture 138: *Attack to the trachea. In order to bring the attacker down, press the fingers downward behind the breastbone.*

Picture 139a: *Signals of helplessness: "What do you want from me?"*
Picture 139b: *After this psychological preparation, a direct attack to the eye. Consider the angle of the hand.*

9.2.4 Palkup-chiki

Elbow techniques are some of the best the close-range weapons! Since these techniques are no long trained or are neglected in regular Taekwondo training, it is necessary to intensively train the different versions of the elbow techniques (see below) with a partner on a heavy bag, on a pad and in different situations.

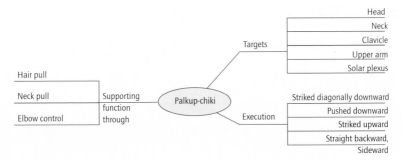

Mindmap 9: *Palkup-chiki*

Picture 140: *Target: face/head.*

Picture 141: *Elbow strike upward. Target: chin/neck.*

Picture 142a: *Pulling back movement in preparation for front elbow strike.*
Picture 142b: *Target areas: clavicle, face, breastbone.*

Picture 143: *Target area: Upper arm, shoulder muscles. This strike can lead to a short term uselessness of the arm and thereby creates possibilities subsequent decisive techniques.*

Picture 144: *Backward elbow strike. The free hand increases the power of the strike.*

Picture 145a: *Block on inside with simultaneous knife-hand counter.*
Picture 145b: *Pulling back movement for side-elbow strike.*
Picture 145c: *Execution of elbow strike.*
Picture 145d: *Elbow strike diagonally upward.*
Picture 145e: *Grabbing the neck with simultaneous elbow strike to the chin / neck.*

9.2.5 Me-jumok-/Sonnal-chiki

The advantage of the hammer fist and knife-hand strikes in self-defense is the low risk of injury while providing great power over a short distance.

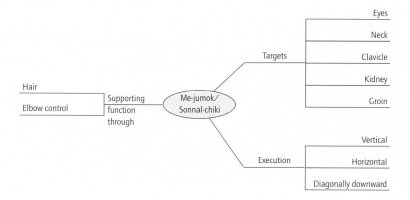

Mindmap 10: *Me-jumok-/Sonnal-chiki*

Picture 146: *Hammer fist to the temple. Movement is the same as Arae-Makki!*

Picture 147: *Knife-hand strike to the neck.*

Picture 148: *Straight knife-hand strike to the clavicle.*

Picture 149: *Hammer fist to the kidneys.*

Picture 150: *Reverse hammer fist to the groin. During execution of strike, the body is turned sharply into the opposite direction.*

Picture 151a: *Attack: Clasping under the arms of the defender.*
Picture 151b: *counter-attack: pulling hair with hammer fist from above.*

PICTURE **152a:** *Block on the inside with simultaneous fingertip strike to the eyes.*
PICTURE **152b:** *The blocking hand transforms into a hammer fist to the angle of the jaw. The attack is pulled through ...*
PICTURE **152c:** *... and becomes a reverse hammer fist to the groin.*
PICTURE **152d:** *The defender turns again to the attacker and strikes with a right hammer fist to the face.*

9.3 Special Techniques

9.3.1 Head Butt

The head butt represents a kind "ultima ratio" in the extreme close distance. Through the weight of the head (approx. 4-4.5 kg) a tremendous effect can be obtained with a head butt. To avoid injuring oneself, however, the front part of the skull must be used to make contact and *not* the forehead!

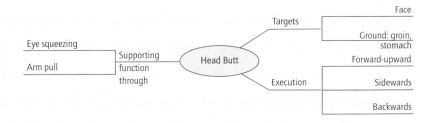

Mindmap 11: *Head Butt*

Picture 153a: *The head of the attacker is controlled with the hands. The forward head butt is a straight, diagonally-upward movement.*
Picture 153b: *In connection with the shoving of the head a translation movement of the entire torso is coupled with a leg extension (= repelling movement).*

Picture 154: *An unorthodox application of the head on the ground! Target area of the head butt is the stomach or the Solar plexus.*

Picture 155a: *Starting position for the backward head butt.*
Picture 155b: *The head butt is executed by throwing the head backwards and extending the body (= pushing the stomach forward).*

Picture 156a: *The attack from above on the inside is blocked with the left hand of the defender. An immediate continuation of the attack is possible by linking with the right arm. In doing so the defender comes to the outside.*

Picture 156b: *The upper arm of the attacker is grabbed with both hands ...*

Picture 156c: *... and is pulled to increase power of the side head butt.*

Picture 157a: *The head butt brings about an overextension of the attacker.*

Picture 157b: *This is exploited by immediately following up with a knee kick to the abdomen.*

9.3.2 "Dirty Tricks"

Under "dirty tricks" we will take a look at the kind of mean techniques which a "respectable" Budoka would normally look down upon. However, these mean techniques can provide the necessary advantage in a conflict and allow the defender to come out of such situations unhurt. For this reason, it is up to the Taekwondo instructor make his students aware of such techniques in self-defense training.

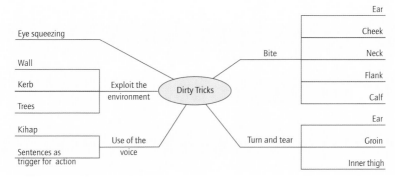

Mindmap 12: *Dirty Tricks*

Picture 158

Picture 159

PICTURE 160

PICTURE 161

PICTURE 162

PICTURE 163: *The inside of the thigh is a very sensitive target. In the shown situation a pinching and twisting leads to the grip around the neck being loosened and thus provides the possibility for the defender to free himself.*

10   Use of the Voice

The voice can be used in various ways in self-defense and provides – when used correctly – the defender with a *tactical advantage*. This tactical advantage is created by *distracting* and/or *steering the attention* of the attacker or by *surprising the opponent*. The defender can ask for example with somewhat confused expression: "What did you say?" or: "Sorry? I did not understand you." A word from the center of this sentence serves as a *trigger*, with which the defender goes into action. The brain of the attacker is "fed" with information, which distracts him from his original intention. Thus the defender has a *time advantage*, which he should use consistently.

Language can also be used in a *de-escalating* way (also and especially because of possible witnesses!). "I do not want any trouble!" and: "Please, leave me alone!" are examples of the *de-escalating function of language in a self-defense situation*. The best way to train this is to combine (*attempted*) *de-escalation with triggers and actions*. These elements must be practiced using *role-plays*, so that they become believable. This also means that greater attention must be dedicated to the integration of these elements in self-defense training before any actual self-defense situation arises!

The use of the *Kihap (= shout)* in a self-defense situation has the following functions:

▸▸ It works as self-motivation and self-instruction.

▸▸ The technique is focused by exhaling explosively, since muscles of the trunk are tensed.

▸▸ A sudden Kihap momentarily shocks the attacker.

It is especially evident in self-defense for woman how difficult it is for the participants to *raise their voices and to become loud*. The use of the voice as an *expression and manifestation of the self-assertion* requires the same amount of training as kicks, strikes and the other elements of self-defense!

11 Visual Awareness of the Defender in Self-defense

In self-defense, a level of perception appropriate to the situation and a continuous flow of information are necessary in order to be able to make a realistic evaluation of the situation. In this context the visual awareness of the defender plays a decisive role. Some of the main questions regarding visual awareness include: "*How* should visual awareness be used?" and: "*What* should be focused on?"

From a physiological point of view, a *constant direction of sight* offers the advantage that the information flow and/or the perception is uninterrupted. If the defender allows his gaze to wander, e.g., he constantly focuses on different points, although from his subjective point of view there are no interruptions to his perception, neuro-physiologically however perception is interrupted in temporal magnitudes which could become dangerous for the defender. Through investigations involving top fencers it emerged that a centralized focus ensures an almost unimpaired flow of information.

The direction of sight must be focused in such a way that all movements of the attacker are perceivable in the peripheral vision of the defender. It is recommended to focus on one point which lies in a triangle between the shoulder and breastbone of the opponent.

Picture 164

12 METHODS OF HEAd CONTROL

The *aspect of control* plays an important role in self-defense. While competition can be considered a kind of combat game (Striking game: I score one point and prevent you from scoring one point on me), this attitude might have fatal consequences in self-defense. In a self-defense situation the defender must gain control over the situation and/or the attacker as quickly as possible. This control in many constellations will be sufficient to deliver – in most cases only one - decisive techniques to end the conflict. If the head is controlled the rest of the body is also under the control of the defender. This refers to both a *mental influence* (attention steering, blocking through foreign stimuli) as well as, quite concretely, a *physical control*. Since the head is the *control center of the body*, the methods of head control should be trained carefully and integrated into the individual repertoire of self-defense techniques. These methods are especially relevant in *close distance* and also partly in *ground fighting*.

These methods will now be demonstrated in detail.

▸▸ *One-handed*

Neck is controlled, followed by knees and elbows.

▸▸ *Diagonally one-handed*

One hand is "hooked" around the neck, the other one is held in a ready position.

▸▸ *Fingertip strike to the eyes*

See chapter 9.2.3 "Pyonsonkut-Chirugi".

▸▸ *Squeezing the eyes with the thumbs*

Hands rest laterally against the head, thumb move to the eyes.

▸▸ *Clinch*

Both hands are around the neck, forearms lie almost parallel, both hands are interlocked, the palms lie on the small point at the back of the head.

Picture 165a
Picture 165b: *The head of the attacker is pulled to his own shoulder or into the elbow.*

a) One hand seizes the knife-hand side of the other.

b) One hand seizes the thumb side of the other.

Picture 166

Picture 167

c) The hands are not folded, as this would prevent them from being pulled apart.

▸▸ *Both hands lie on one side of the head*
From this position the head can be pulled into a side or semicircular knee kick.

▸▸ *One hand on the head, the other around the neck*
Good starting position for a jerky down pull of the head.

PICTURE 168

PICTURE 169

▸▸ *Diagonal hand controls the neck, the other one controls the elbow*

PICTURE 170

PICTURE 171

▸▸ *Claw hand to the Adam's apple, other hand pulls the hair*
▸▸ *Hair pull*
▸▸ *Choke hold (groundwork)*

13 Self-defense against a Weapon

As soon as weapons are introduced into a conflict, this means that the attacker has the *intention of injuring and/or killing*. This requires absolute resoluteness and determination on the part of the defender and it also justifies the use of the hardest means possible in order to defend himself!

The best option – if the possibility exists – is to avoid a conflict or in other words: to run away!

There are – as always in self-defense – no winners. *The defender must always be prepared for the fact that he could be hurt!* This fact must be emphasized over and over during *mental preparation* (also a part of self-defense training!). In this context the *aspect of the self-preservation* takes on even greater significance than in self-defense against an unarmed opponent.

As an example of the arsenal of weapons nowadays used on the streets, we will now look at sticks/baseball bats, chains and knives.

13.1 Sticks/Baseball Bats

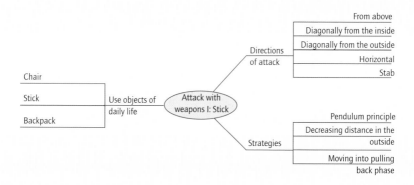

Mindmap 13: *Attack with weapons I: Stick*

Sticks/baseball bats are weapons which increase the *reach of the user* as well as his striking power. The dangerous part of the weapon is near the end where the highest speed and striking power is reached. The main question regarding self-defense against sticks/baseball bats is therefore: How do I get out from the range of the end of the weapon?

The *striking paths* of the stick/baseball bat are usually *circular* or *curved*. Stabbing movements (target: face, larynx, Solar plexus, abdomen) and *strikes with the stick/baseball bat held with two hands* are also possible. Here we will primarily discuss defense against attacks from a circular path, since these occur most frequently in practice.

The defender has two *main problems*:

▸▸ Exact estimation of distance.
▸▸ Anticipation of the attack angle (which direction will the strike come from?).

The *following basic strategies* come into play:

▸▸ Moving out of the line of the circle drawn by the point of the weapon, and as soon as the point has gone past initiate a counter-attack.

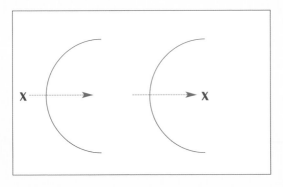

Figure 7

▸▸ Moving into the pulling back movement (= "into the circle"). Here the defender is confronted with the *problem of exact timing*.

Both strategies should be used in the training.

Firstly, the different possible *paths of attack* of a stick/baseball bat should be worked on in training *in slow motion*.

Training exercises could include *moving out of the reach of the stick/baseball bat whilst remaining as close as possible to the attacker or practicing moving into the anticipated arc at the correct moment* and thus neutralizing the effect of the weapon. As soon as the student is used to the range of the weapon, the speed, of the attacks should be increased. Both principles – *pendulum principle* and *moving directly into the attack* – should also be trained with sticks/baseball bats of *different lengths* in order to train the estimation of distance.

The defender should not to try to stop a strike but to *divert* the attack since even successfully blocking the blow could lead to serious injury due to the weight of the weapon.

SElEcTEd ExAMplES of DEfENSE AGAiNST Stick/BASEbAll BAT

The attacker is right-handed.

PicTuRE 172a-b

PICTURE 173a-b

PICTURE 174a-b

Picture 175a-b

When training with weapons it is advisable to use protective equipment as this provides safety to participants – also when practizing the realistic use of the weapons. In doing this, patterns of movements are trained which can be used in real situations.

Helmets with full visor are suitable for the training of self-defense against the stick, like those kindly provided to us by the company KUNTAO (see Appendix 2).

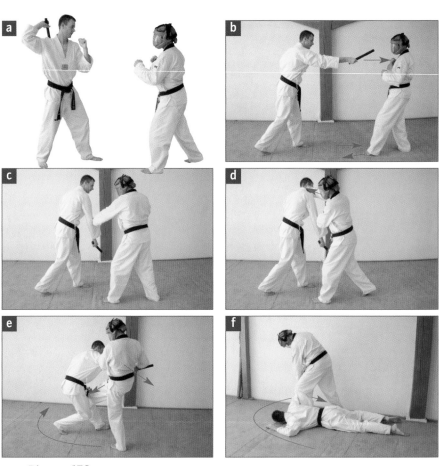

Picture 176a

Picture 176b: *With this defense method the pendulum principle is used. This means that the defender goes as far out of the range of the weapon that it barely misses him.*

Picture 176c: *This is followed directly an elbow control technique with the left hand...*

Picture 176d: *... followed by a punch to the head. The striking hand is used to control the stick arm of the attacker.*

Picture 176e: *This is followed by a stop kick to the inside of the left knee combined with a pull of the weapon arm of the attacker.*

Picture 176f: *The defender goes in to a two-step 180° turn and continues the lock to the ground.*

Continued on the next page

PICTURE 177a: *In contrast to the previous sequence, contact is directly established between the right arm of the defender and the attack arm.*

PICTURE 177b: *Through the early establishment of contact the stretched right contact arm plays the role of a kind of crash barrier, i.e. the attack slides past the defender.*

PICTURE 177c: *Using a two-step turn with simultaneous elbow control the defender positions himself side-on to the attacker on the outside.*

PICTURE 177d: *counter-attack with punch to the face.*

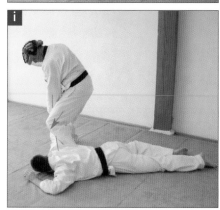

Picture 177e: *Pulling back for the second punch.*

Picture 177f: *Execution of punch. The striking hand seizes the wrist of the weapon arm.*

Picture 177g: *Two-step turn whilst applying lock.*

Picture 177h: *Securing the attacker to the ground with the knee.*

Picture 177i: *Securing on the ground.*

PICTURE 178a: *The defender moves into the directly attack with a block and finger claw to the eyes.*

PICTURE 178b: *The attack arm is fixed under left armpit and the opponent is overcome by permanent pressure to the eyes.*

PICTURE 178c: *The weapon arm remains fixed under the left armpit.*

PICTURE 178d: *The head of the attacker is controlled with the left knee. From this position there are many different possibilities for a final technique and the removal of the weapon.*

Picture 179a: *Stick attack from the side. The defender moves directly into the attack and blocks the weapon arm.*

Picture 179b: *The pressure on the eyes with the fingertips of the right hand is maintained. This is followed by a throw (outer crescent).*

Picture 179c: *Preparing to remove the weapon.*

Picture 179d: *Weapon removal with knee kick downward to the head of the attacker.*

If any objects are at hand, they should be used when defending against weapons. Such objects could include: chair, scarf, key ring, overhanging roof beams etc (see Chapter 14 "The Use of Everyday Objects as Weapons").

Picture 180a: *The stick attack is stopped in the early phase by a chair leg.*

Picture 180b: *The chair is thrown to the side then the attacker is seized with an elbow and head control on the closest and then, with a two-step turn, is thrown head-first into the wall. (Remember: Use the environment as your friend. This is to be integrated systematically into training and practiced purposefully.)*

Picture 180c: *Possible follow up techniques: Knee and elbow.*

PICTURE 181a: *During the pulling back phase, a strike with a chair leg is directed towards the face of the attacker.*

PICTURE 181b: *The sharp movement to the face causes a reaction in the attacker where his eyes close automatically.*

PICTURE 181c: *The chair is thrown to the side and the defender positions himself on the outside of the attacker.*

PICTURE 181d: *Control of the attack arm, finger strike to the eye.*

PICTURE 181e: *The attacker is brought to ground.*
PICTURE 181f: *Punch to the head.*
PICTURE 181g: *Disarmament.*
PICTURE 181h

Picture 182a: *Use of backpack.*
Picture 182b: *Impairing vision of attacker.*
Picture 182c: *Head and elbow control.*
Picture 182d: *Knee kick to the abdomen.*
Picture 182e: *Securing the attack arm while executing diagonally downward elbow strike. Possibilities for continuation by using a throw and / or further strikes and kicks are given.*

Picture 183a: *Stick against stick.*
Picture 183b: *Block and simultaneous stick counter-attack to the elbow joint.*
Picture 183c: *Continuation into strike to the thigh.*
Picture 183d: *Strike against the face.*

Picture 184a: *"Crash barrier".*
Picture 184b: *Elbow control and step turn to the outside with simultaneous strike with stick to the wrist of the attacker.*
Picture 184c: *While maintaining control of elbow sideward stick strike to the head of the attacker.*
Picture 184d: *Application of lock.*

13.2 Chains

For the defense against the chain the use of the pendulum principle is preferred, since this weapon, once deflected, is less manoeuvrable than a stick. Estimating the exact distance is more problematic than with attacks with a stick, as it is very difficult to judge the length of a (folded) chain. Possible training weapons include plastic barricade chains from building sites or climbing ropes.

Examples of Application

Picture 185a
Picture 185b: *Twisting out of attack.*
Picture 185c: *After the attack passes the defender rapidly throws punches to the head of the attacker.*
Picture 185d-e

13.3   Knives

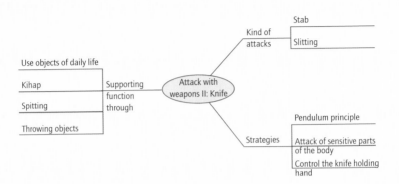

Mindmap 14: *Attack with weapons II: Knife*

The knife holds a *privileged position* in the family of weapons. It is small, extremely manoeuvrable and – in the hands of a trained user – absolutely lethal. While it is possible to seize the previously discussed weapons when defending this is impossible to do with a knife. If objects which can be employed as a *weapon* or *shield* are at hand they should be put to use. The fighting stance used in knife defense differs from the usual stance. The attacker will only be offered the sides of the arms with the extensor tendons. The reason for this is that even if the tendons are injured or severed, the defender still has the *ability to bend* his hand i.e. he can still use his fingers to *grab*. If the flexor tendons are severed the hand is rendered useless for self-defense. The defender must be aware of the fact that, due to the effects of adrenalin, that he might not notice possible injuries until later. After a conflict the defender must therefore examine himself very thoroughly!

The conventional self-defense principle of: "one knife attack – one defense" is completely unrealistic! The attacks consist of a *mixture of stabs, cuts and slicing movements*, accompanied or preceded by *kicks* and/or *attempts to restrain with the free hand*.

The aim of the defense must be to keep the attacker at a distance by using *quick, mobile leg work* and *low kicks* until a possibility to control the knife holding hand appears. This control – if it happens once – should under no circumstances be given up!

Self-defense training against knife attacks is extremely frustrating because it is constantly emphasized how vulnerable one is when defending against a knife!

Remember: Anyone who attacks with a knife, no matter whether it is man, woman or child, is a potentially lethal opponent and must be treated and regarded as such! Underestimation of an opponent will lead to injury and/or death!

EXAMPLES OF APPLICATION

PICTURE 186: *Notice the protective glasses of the defender and the defense position with the extensor tendon side of the forearms turned to the attacker.*

PICTURE 187a: *Stab attack.*
PICTURE 187b: *Slicing movement.*

PICTURE 188a

PICTURE 188b: *The stab attack is evaded.*

PICTURE 188c: *The knife arm is controlled.*

PICTURE 188d: *A stop kick sideward to the knee joint follows.*

PICTURE 188e: *Application of hand lock.*
PICTURE 188f: *Attacker is secured using hand lock.*
In principle locks result from the situation. One should never aim to use these as a final technique! When fighting against a knife the probability of being able to apply a lock is extremely small!! The main means of defense to be used are distance regulation, strikes and kicks!

PICTURE 189a: *The defender throws an object (folder, key ring, purse etc.) to the face of the attacker.*

PICTURE 189b: *This fast movement toward the eyes causes a reflex action in the eyelids which forces them to close.*

PICTURE 189c: *The defender uses the short moment of disorientation of the attacker to move in and take control of the attacker's knife hand.*

PICTURE 189d: *A stop kick with the foot edge into the knee joint of the attacker follows.*

PICTURE 189e: *Following on from this the counter action is continued with a shin kick to the groin.*

PICTURE 189f: *Application of lock.*

PICTURE 189g: *Securing on the ground.*

PICTURE 189h: *Disarmament.*

A similar sequence from another perspective:

Picture 190a-d

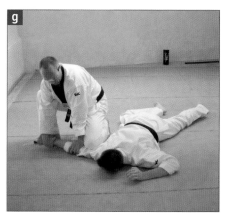

PICTURE 190e-h

14 The Use of Everyday Objects as Weapons

In a self-defense situation it can be very helpful to use the everyday objects usually carried around as weapons. In doing this the effect of unarmed techniques can be increased. Additionally a surprise effect is caused through the use of an object in an "unconventional" way. This chapter does not discuss all the different possibilities of using everyday objects as weapons. The aim of the chapter is rather to point out possibilities and provide food for thought to help individual students to integrate his own "everyday weapons" into his personal self-defense. The following everyday objects are very useful and when used correctly can function as weapons.

14.1 Book/Briefcase

When held with either one or two hands a book can be used as a striking weapon. The defender should try to strike with a corner or an edge.

PICTURE 191

14.2 Rolled-up Newspaper

A rolled-up newspaper can be used like a baton for striking and pushing.

Example of use:

Picture 192a: *Gesture of helplessness, signal lack of understanding. The rolled-up newspaper is held inconspicuously in the hand.*
Picture 192b: *The attempt to seize the defender is diverted.*
Picture 192c: *Strike to the neck.*
Picture 192d: *The strike is directly continued horizontally to the face.*
Picture 192e: *This strike causes an overstretching of the attacker, which is gratefully exploited by the defender who fires a shin kick to the abdomen.*

14.3 Pen/Pencil

A pen can be used to *increase pressure* on sensitive points.

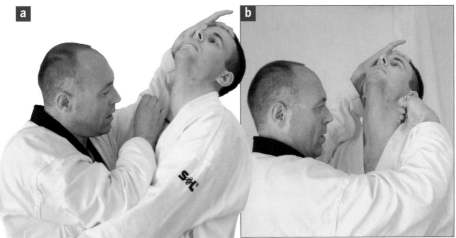

Picture 193a: *Trachea.*
Picture 193b: *Pit of clavicle.*
Picture 193c: *Eye.*
Picture 193d: *Bend of the elbow.*

14.4 KEYS

Keys are to be used mainly as stabbing and "slicing" weapons.

If a Taekwondoka decides to integrate these everyday weapons into his self-defense repertoire then he must ask himself the following questions:

▸▸ Can the object be accessed quickly?

▸▸ How does the use of this object fit in with my other self-defense techniques?
The use of an everyday weapon must not hinder the use of other techniques.

▸▸ Am I sufficiently experienced in using this everyday weapon?
The lack of training can lead to the weapon being used on me!

PICTURE 194: *Holding a key.*

PICTURE 195a-b

15 METHODICAL SEQUENCE for dealing with Self-defense Situations

The sequence suggested here for introducing and dealing with self-defense situations is not to be understood in such a way that it is totally necessary to go through each step in order to be successful. Whether the instructor goes through each step, depends among other things on time, technical repertoire, learning speed and the previous knowledge of the students. The idea of this methodical sequence is to help the students to understand as many important aspects of a self-defense situation as possible. This includes theoretical knowledge and knowledge of variations, possibilities to disrupt and one's own limits. In this respect, this sequence can be regarded as a kind of "quarry" from which the instructor can take stones to "build a house" according to the individual requirements of the student.

Define the Situation

Determining of distance; kind of attack; having a model idea of the path of the attack; Cross references to similar situations, in order to work out classes of attack.

Work on Functions of Attacks

Often the students will have no clear idea on how an attack looks in reality. Attacks with basic techniques, which will never occur on the street, shouldn't occur in self-defense training either! The bad habit of stopping an attack too early or leaving it standing, creates a false internal model in the student.

Point out technical Options for the Neutralization of Attacks

Run through all phases of a self-defense situation; if necessary, limit this to 1-2 phases, but then fit these into the entire chain of action.

Be able to justify each action!

Slowing down of Execution of Techniques in Comparison with Real-time

Examination on the basis the *parameters*

▸▸ Functionality of the attack.
▸▸ Distance.
▸▸ Position.
▸▸ Timing.
▸▸ Motor solution with regard to control, self-preservation, completeness.

Increase Intensity

The *speed* of attack is *increased* (getting closer to real-time), the *power* of the attack is *increased*.

When techniques are executed safely the frequency of attacks should be increased (attacking in a row, circle).

Including disrupting Elements (defined by Instructor)

The previous stages in the sequence are carried out with cooperative partners, i.e. the partners make it possible for each other to get an idea and feeling of the complete (and uninterrupted) range of movements and to *always* complete a movement. Through the use of disrupting elements the student will become aware of "breaks" in a self-defense situation and his adaptability is trained. In addition the student learns to *always* continue an action to the end, regardless of whether it is the one he started or another dictated by disrupting elements.

Aim of this stage: Adaptability to changing situations and resoluteness.

Single Possibility for Attack

There are two possibilities for attacking *within the same distance*. The aim of this step is the link between recognizing the attack in the early stages (= perception training) and choosing the appropriate self-defense chain of action. The intensity of this exercise is increased if *attacks from different distances* are available.

Various Possibilities for Attack

The same concepts as those for single possibility for attack also apply here. The difference is, however, that the degree of the uncertainty is increased by 3-5 possible attacks.

Free Attacks

The defender has no idea at all of the distance and kind of the attack. In this stage variations in intensity are also possible (e.g. slow motion attacks, indicated attacks through defender starting early, under time pressure against a row or in the circle).

Handicap Training

Handicap training means that the defender has to operate under certain restrictive conditions, e. g.:

▶▶ Limited vision (one eye is covered).
▶▶ No advance warning (surprise attacks).
▶▶ Limited use of extremities (using only the right arm for the defense, the whole left half of the body is defined as being injured etc.).
▶▶ Limited space (telephone boxes, the back to the wall, the corner of a room).
▶▶ Time pressure (rapid series of attacks from different opponents).
▶▶ Dealing with pain (learning "to take a punch" without it affecting the self-defense capabilities).
▶▶ Restrictive clothing (tight jeans, heavy coat, with backpack).
▶▶ Different environments (stairs, in an apartment with furniture as obstacles, different surfaces such as grass, sand, carpet etc.).
▶▶ Bad light (candle, strobe light).

Concerning timing, the unit of defense/counter technique can be executed in three different ways.

Successively

I.e. first the defense is executed and then the counter technique takes place. This sequence is used in the model fighting systems of Taekwondo. The advantage is in the level of power achieved with each individual component and the concentration of the student on the respective technique. In self-defense, however, the unfavorable time structure is to be considered, i.e., the sequence is simply too slow. This changes if basic defensive techniques are used as offensive movements against joints and other parts of the body of the attacker. In this respect it can be seen as having a supporting function regarding the final, decisive technique.

PICTURE **196a**: *Block.*
PICTURE **196b**: *Counter.*

PICTURE **197a-b**

In the previous sequence a successive defense and counter technique are used, but through the use of the same arm for the block and the counter it comes the time structure is shortened. The block is changed without delay into a fingertip strike to the eye.

PICTURE 198a-d

To above sequence: After the defender has caught the kicking leg of the attacker, a counter-attack to the face of the attacker takes place followed directly by a classic Arae-Makki technique to the knee joint of the attacker. The "block" presents itself here as a decisive final offensive technique.

PICTURE 199a-c

SimulTANEOusly

A simultaneous block and counter places greater coordinative requirements on the Taekwondoka than the above-mentioned, more commonly trained variant. The advantage is the reduction in time of the entire action. Preference should be given to this variant in Hosinsul training.

PICTURE 200

Picture 201

Prematurely

With a well-developed sense of anticipation and the appropriate speed it is possible to execute a technique into the attack of the opponent, before the attack is completed. The defense exists only in the form of a guard for self-preservation. From a technical point of view this is certainly the most elegant solution, from a legal point of view, however, the premature counter technique could be seen as an attack (problem: witnesses who do not understand the situation!). This could mean a reversal of the actual sequence of events – with the corresponding legal consequences.

Conclusion from the above-mentioned factors regarding self-defense training practice:

▸▸ The training of basic blocking techniques as offensive techniques
▸▸ The preference of a simultaneous block and counter technique whilst taking into account control and self-preservation.

16 PRACTICE: TRAINING EXERCISES TO SIMULATE different SITUATIONS

The exercise forms described here are to represent an enrichment of conventional training. The coordinative requirements to successfully overcome the self-defense situation are greatly different from those of the Dojang. The descriptions of the exercises have been kept very brief as they should serve to provide ideas to the instructor and to leave enough room for notes, ideas and additions for students.

16.1 Emphasis: Environmental Handicaps

Grass, Sand, uneven Ground

If possible, train outside on different surfaces. Analyze what is possible and what is not!

Uphill, downhill

Through the changed position of the targets (higher, lower) the techniques must be adapted to the given conditions. Kicks uphill or downhill e.g. must be balanced differently than on a level surface.

Upstairs, downstairs

Generally, the same rules as for point 2 said can be applied here but things are made more difficult because of the lack of continuity of the ground. Training should be done with appropriate caution to prevent students from injury. Use step aerobic steps!

Training in a full Room

Furniture, laundry mountains and carpet folds are conditions which must be integrated into self-defense strategies. Each student must work out a set of techniques which can be applied and are effective even under these handicaps!

Bad Light

Too bright = > looking into the sun, half-light, strobe light (Disco!).

Limited Space

Corners of a room, crowds, telephone boxes, and narrow bars are only some examples of situations which can be simulated in training.

16.2 Emphasis: Personal handicaps

Clothing

Clothes which are too tight, winter clothes, backpack on the back.

Limited Vision

One covered, both eyes closed (good exercise form for the ground!).

Physical Handicaps

Certain extremities are not to be used, e.g. the left arm is fixed to the Dobok or in the belt.

16.3 Emphasis: Defender has only one Opportunity to Counter-attack

The defender has only one opportunity to counter. This one opportunity is worked out by using stepping, a good guard and evading.

16.4 Emphasis: Prediction

Decide on one technique and use only this technique to counter.

16.5   Emphasis: Power

Heavy-bag Training

Rounds of 1-2 minutes, especially using techniques such as knees and elbow.

Arm Pads

At the moment of the impact, the pad holder presses the pad strongly into the technique.

Three-way Uchi-Komi

This form of exercise is taken from judo. One partner secures himself on the belt and/or at the clothes to prevent the other student from throwing. The student now tries, using all his power, to throw and to bring the secured partner to the ground.

Picture 202a-d.

16.6 Emphasis: Dealing with Pain

The bad news is that realistic self-defense training will always involved some level of pain (in the opinion of the authors). The good news is that a gradual habituation is possible through sensible training. Regardless of technical ability and psychological strength, if dealing with pain is not trained, there is a great risk of becoming incapacitated in a conflict – even from a less serious – strike. The more protected the environment where in which the average Central European moves, the more he is sheltered from the necessity of having to assert himself in dangerous situations. Although thought of having to expose yourself to strikes may be unpleasant, there is no other way if the aim is to be able to continue fighting despite pain.

The Three-man-drill

One partner stands in the middle with one partner in front and another partner behind. The partner in the middle is attacked and hit with low kicks, Ap-Chagi etc. and he then counters directly with 1-2 techniques, without being distracted by the effect of the hit.

PICTURE 203a-j

DUMMY GAME

One partner is "the human punch bag" for the other one and consciously allows himself be hit. The training of the reflective trunk musculature, sharp exhaling and covering guarding is the aim of this exercise.

16.7   Emphasis: Control

A good rule of thumb for the use of the hands in self-defense is as follows: one hand is used to control, the other one strikes or does other mean, disgusting things. Two-handed control grips serve to create positions and possibilities from which other techniques can be executed. Basically, the purpose of control grips is, for a short time, to limit the opponent in what he can do. In the exercises introduced here the time interval is artificially lengthened, which on one hand is quite unrealistic, but on the other hand it helps the students to develop a feeling for the possibilities and limits of control.

One-handed Control Grips

▶▶ Elbow control.
▶▶ Neck control.

Two-handed Control Grasps

▶▶ Clinch - four forms.
▶▶ Combined elbow and neck control.

These exercises are done for 30-40 seconds with a partner who is either cooperative and only resists slightly or who resists completely (depending upon ability of the student). Each partner does 3-5 repetitions.

16.8   Emphasis: Several Opponents

Dealing with several opponents should be practiced in different constellations, one of which should be an emergency assistance situation.

1 vs. 2

Strategies: To get to the flank, so that an opponent can not directly get to the defender.

PICTURE 204a-g

Picture 205a-c
Picture 205d: *After a two-step turn attacker Nr.1 stands as a shield between the defender and attacker Nr. 2.*
Picture 205e-g

1 vs. 3

The three opponents are dealt with like two opponents, which means that the defender tries to get to the flank and to get one of the attackers between himself and the others. Moving between the attackers should be avoided.

2 vs. 1 (Emergency Assistance)

In role plays aimed at practicing emergency assistance situations, the person providing the help should concentrate on preserving his own safety as well as bringing wildly, lashing-out opponents under control.

2 vs. 2

This variation should also be trained.

2 vs. 3

Relatively speaking, this constellation is nothing more than a combination of 1:1, 1:2, 2:1. The special attraction of this exercise the individual constellations can flow into one another.

Every Man for himself (3-6 Participants)

The attraction of this exercise is that the defender must constantly adjust to different situations. Some possible situations include one defender having to contend with several opponents and completely confusing constellations which bring about total chaos.

16.9   Emphasis: Ground Fighting

Obtaining ground fighting capabilities such as those of, for example, a Judoka is not the aim of Taekwondo self-defense. The questions to be covered are rather: How does my technique change, if I am forced to fight on the ground? Which techniques are at all still possible at the ground?

The aim is not, like it would be in judo, to apply a stranglehold, a lock or a hold but to get in to a position which makes it possible for the defender to use strong and efficient techniques despite limited and unusual circumstances. This positioning on the ground is the focus of the following exercise forms.

Side-on Positioning

Four starting positions of the attacker.
Aim: Side-on positioning of the defender.

Diagonal Arm

Picture 206a-b

Defender on Ground => Standing up despite being obstructed by Opponent

See chapter 6.4. "Self-defense from the Ground".

Pad Training on the Ground

From a position on the ground is difficult for the defender to obtain maximum striking and kicking power since he cannot use certain muscles which usually play an important role in developing power from a standing position. Despite this deficiency, he has to develop the greatest power possible whilst on the ground to avoid wasting his energy on ineffective actions.

PICTURE **207a:** *Due to the positioning of the legs around the hips of the pad holder the defender is only able to use the twisting of the trunk and the extension of the arm to generate power.*
PICTURE **207b**

PICTURE **208a:** *The pad is grabbed to simulation pulling the neck or hair.*
PICTURE **208b**

Picture 209a: *Pulling back for a knee kick from the ground.*
Picture 209b: *Gaining power by pulling the arms into the kick and which activates the abdominal muscles.*

Picture 210a-d

PICTURE 211a-d

16.10 Emphasis: Positioning

Positioning in self-defense means that the defender tries to get to the outside or to the back of the attacker. Simply moving backwards can have fatal consequences, since the defender remains within the attacking range of the attacker.

PICTURE 212a-c

Picture 213a-b

Diagonal Evasion

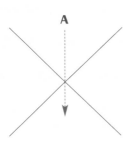

A

Lines of orientation lines are marked on the ground. The defender stands center of the crossing lines of the X, the attacker stands in front of him.

Figure 8

Back to the Wall

Due to the danger posed by this situation the defender must evade to the side or diagonally forward.

PICTURE 214a: *Head of the attacker into the wall.*
PICTURE 214b: *Hook to the solar plexus.*

Two-step Turn

The defender stands with the back to the wall. By control of one side of the attacker's body and a two-step turn he can pin the attacker to the wall.

PICTURE 215a
PICTURE 215b: *The defender starts a two-step turn away from the wall and takes control of the right side of the attacker at the elbow and neck.*
PICTURE 215c

PICTURE 215d: *The attacker is pushed into the wall.*
PICTURE 215e: *Continuation with left elbow strike to the head.*
PICTURE 215f: *Left knee kick to the inner thigh of the attacker.*
PICTURE 215g: *Right elbow diagonally upward to the face of the attacker.*

Training on the Inside of the Attacker

It is not always possible to land directly on the outside of the attacker. Since the defender is, however, in reach of the extremities of the attacker when he is on the inside, a coupling (= simultaneous) of blocking technique and counter-attack is necessary in order to get to the outside.

16.11 Emphasis: Timing

Delayed Attack

The instructor gives the signal to attack, which should not happen immediately but sometime within 15-20 seconds. The advantage of this exercise is the constant factor of uncertainty.

"Trigger Word Training"

Each student keeps a sentence ready as which can be used in reaction to a threat. A word from this sentence serves as trigger to the counter-attack. E.g.: "What did you say?", whereby the word "you" acts as the trigger. No matter how ridiculous one might feel at the beginning, this training is very important as it distracts the attention of the attacker and he can then be caught off-guard by a follow-up technique.

Training under Time Pressure

A student stands in a circle or facing in a row. The attackers come quickly one after the other in a manner that leaves no time for the defender to consciously consider his actions. Above all, the row is suitable for attaining frequencies of attack (with, to a large extent, strong techniques on side of the defender). The circle form of this exercise offers more options for variation:

- ▸▸ Attacks in a clockwise direction.
- ▸▸ Attacks in a counter-clockwise direction.
- ▸▸ Attacking on signal.

▸▸ Attackers are given numbers before the exercise = > attacks take place from appropriate attacker when his number is called.

▸▸ Spectrum of possible attacks ranges from given techniques to free attacks.

Hidden Signal

The partners line-up in two rows, facing one another. The instructor stands behind the defenders and gives a visual signal to attack.

16.12   Emphasis: Resoluteness

Experience shows that in self-defense it is mostly choreographed sequences with 1-2 counter techniques to an attack which are taught. If this is sufficient in a conflict situation – great!

If not – and this is mostly the case – the defender will very quickly run out of ideas. The aim of the exercises, which train resoluteness in the counter-attacking, is to really continue a self-defense action all the way to its end (in the sense of an optimal solution!).

Redundancy Training

Each attack is essentially answered with 3-5 techniques. Attention should be paid to correctness and efficiency!

Five-distances Training

Techniques from all five distances are used. All five distances are gone through, so that the exercise ends on the ground.

Role-play

Verbal escalation and de-escalation should be integrated into exercises. The exercise should be run through from trigger word up to the neutralization of the attacker.

Willpower Training on the Ground

One partner tightly holds the legs of the defender on the ground and lays top of him. A second partner chokes or holds. The defender tries with all his strength to free himself. This should last for 2-3 repetitions of 30-40 seconds each. Very demanding!

Picture 216a-b

16.13   Emphasis: Regulating Distance

Increasing Distance

Partner attacks with given or free techniques. The defender extends the distance in such a way that his opponent misses him by a hair's breadth. The aim of this exercise is to learn to be able to judge distance exactly.

Decreasing Distance

Move into the attack, before it has been fully executed. This means to shorten reacting and shortening the distance to the attacker at the slightest indication of an attack. This is done best in connection with close-combat techniques such as knees and elbows (possibly also the head).

16.14   Emphasis: Reaction Time

General reaction time is, to large extent, genetically defined. In these exercises the reaction to moving stimuli is trained.

▸▸ One partner stands facing the wall at a distance of 3-6m. The smaller this distance, the more demanding the exercise will be. The other partner stands at a distance of 2-3m behind him and throws a ball (e.g. a tennis ball) at the wall. Partner no. 1 should try

- to catch the ball.
- to hit the ball with a pre-defined fixed foot technique.
- to hit the ball with the fist.

PICTURE 217a-d

One variation of this exercise is that in the beginning both partners stand facing each other. Right after the ball has been thrown the executing partner rapidly turns to the wall.

- One partner stands upon a chair or a bench etc.. His outstretched hand holds a ball (e.g. tennis ball), which he suddenly drops. The other partner has the same task as in the exercise described above.

Appendix

Appendix 1 – Recommended Reading

Every recommended reading list has a slight hint of subjectivity to it. This is also the case here. Self-defense can be compared to building a house. Taekwondo and all other martial arts form a kind of quarry which supplies raw materials. Everyone should choose "stones" from the available "building material" which are relevant to their own self-defense, their character and their physique. The intention of this book was to demonstrate the criteria for selecting effective "building blocks"! Look over the fence, take on what is suitable and be open to new things! If our book has given you the impetus to do these things then it has fulfilled its purpose!

Anderson, Dan
American Freestyle Karate
A Guide to Sparring
Hollywood, CA 1980

Beasley, Jerry
In Search of the Ultimate Martial Art
The Jeet Kune Do Experience
Boulder, CO 1989

Beasley, Jerry
The Way of no Way
Solving the Jeet Kune Do Riddle
Boulder, CO 1992

Choi, Hong Hi
Taekwon-Do
The Art of Self-defense
Seoul, Korea 1965

Christensen, Loren W.
Fighter's Fact Book
Wetherfield, CT 2000

Hanho
Combat Strategy
Junsado: The Way of the Warrior
Wetherfields, CT 1992

Hartsell, Larry
Jeet Kune Do
Entering to Trapping to Grappling
Burbank, CA 1984

Hirneise, Lothar & Pertl, Klaus
Quo vadis Ving Tsun
Modern Views on an Ancient System
Kernen 1988

Jones Greg
Predator Training
The Inner Beast of San Soo
Boulder, CO 1993

Kent, Chris & Tackett Tim
Jun Fan / Jeet Kune Do
The Textbook
Los Angeles, CA 1988

Lovret, Fredrick J.
The Way and the Power
Secrets of Japanese Strategy
Boulder, CO 1987

Rabesa, Arthur
Kumite
The Complete Fighting Text
Brockton, MA 1984

Sde-Or, Juri & Yanilov, Eyal
Krav Maga
How to Defend Yourself against Armed Assault
Tel Aviv 2001

Vunak, Paul
Jeet Kune Do
Its Concept and Philosophies
Burbank, CA o. J.

Appendix 2 – List of Sources

We would like to thank the company S+L Sportartikel GmbH for providing us with the hard-wearing doboks. Even after putting them the under the hardest of strain, they were still in tip-top condition!

The company Kuntao Martial Arts Equipment who provided us with the protective equipment and training weapons. The protection offered by these articles allowed us to demonstrate our techniques as realistically as possible.

S + L Sportartikel GmbH
Elisabethstraße 42
D-40217 Duesseldorf
Germany
Fon: +49 (211) 37 08 74
Fax: +49 (211) 37 09 08
eMail: slsport@t-online.de

Fa. KUNTAO
Holger Morell
Hauptstr. 154
D-97299 Zell am Main
Germany
Fon: +49 (01 77) 2 78 28 19
eMail: kuntao@t-online.de
URL: www.kuntao.de

Photo & Illustration Credits

Cover Design: B. Engelen
Cover photo: J. Vetter, M. Dautzenberg
Photos: M. Dautzenberg

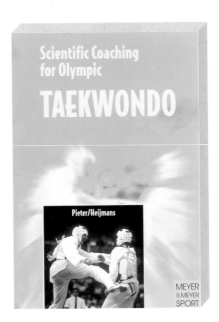

Pieter/Heijmans
Scientific Coaching
for Olympic Taekwondo

After many years of scientific studies the authors present the first publication on systematic training in taekwondo, based on scientific principles. Next to a chapter on the anatomy of joints, the reader will find systematic information on all the aspects of training such as periodization, training endurance, strength training, technical, psychological and tactical training for competition. The book closes with a chapter on injuries in taekwondo, with their prevention and special training for injured athletes.

2nd edition
248 pages, 90 photos, 45 figures
Paperback, 5³/4″ x 8 ¹/4″
ISBN 1-84126-047-9
£ 12.95 UK/$ 17.95 US
$ 25.95 CDN/€ 18.90

Anz Taekwondo 12/03

MEYER & MEYER Sport | sales@m-m-sports.com | www.m-m-sports.com